Essential Survival for Everyone

By Nick Eager

Copyright 2022 Nick Eager

* * * * *

Introduction

Humans are very resourceful. We can survive in any environment with enough knowledge. You can find solutions to survive.

In most disasters, your biggest priority is shelter. You can survive only three hours in a blizzard without shelter, but you can survive three days without water, and three weeks without food. This guide can be used for temporary disruptions such as a local disaster. However, most people will never be lost in the woods or in a major disaster. Many survival books focus on that being lost in the woods. The main purpose of this book is to rebuild quality of life after a significant disruption to the normal way of living.

The guide assumes that problems have come on suddenly. There are some scenarios where you need to know what to do with no warning, so this is most useful for that situation. However, big changes often happen slowly. If you have warning, time, and resources to prepare, there are many more things that you could do. The priorities are the same as discussed here but having time might allow you to make the transition go much more smoothly. For example, in the dry west, water may be a bigger challenge. I recommend storing only a month of supplies or maybe more if you live farther north. However, if you had warning that you'd need it, there is no reason not to go all out stocking up. Read at least the section on short-term survival because preparation for that is easy and makes a huge difference. The other sections can be read when you need it if you have a hard copy.

This guide is not meant to replace what you do now. These instructions are for when no other options are available. For example, the health guidelines here assume that no emergency rooms or medical doctors are available.

All areas of the world have food that can be found. That food isn't often the favored types of food, but it is often healthier. In most areas there is enough food to support large populations, but the food isn't always right outside the front door. This guide focuses on food in the U.S. and Canada, but many of the skills for finding food are useful elsewhere.

Short-Term

Shelter and Protection

A cold winter rain can be deadly in minutes for an unprotected person. Keeping dry is of utmost importance. The options below should help protect you. If you are in a house, no matter the condition, it will be enough for the short term. The temperature is not likely to drop or climb so quickly that you can't live there until you have a better plan. Flood, storm, and fire are things that could make you move immediately. Among those, only fire is something you have control over, so be careful.

Field shelters

Being lost in a blizzard is extremely rare, but still, it could happen. In a blizzard with snow already on the ground, snow is a great insulator, so use it. You could bury yourself in snow up to your face. You could dig a hole in a drift to make a cave. Start a cave low and dig up so that warm air stays trapped. You only need a small hole to provide fresh air. If your breathing becomes labored, make the hole bigger. Staying dry is equally important.

If you have time to make a shelter, you can make it from whatever is available. For example, a rope between trees or leaning branches can provide a structure to lay foliage on. If they are dry, reed grasses like cattails or phragmites can be quickly snapped off by hand and piled over a structure.

Watch the weather. Be wary when you see changes in the wind and clouds that are lowering and increasing.

Weather

Cirrus clouds are very high clouds. Most commonly they are stratus which is flat. Cumulus clouds have flat bases and domed tops.

When there are clear skies, rapidly changing weather is not likely. If it is hot and humid, it will likely get hotter before it cools. If it is winter, clear skies at night means dropping temperatures, especially if snow is on the ground. Having a few scattered cumulus clouds often means fair weather. Also, having a few wispy cirrus clouds could mean fair to cold weather.

"Mackerel sky, not three days dry." Cirrocumulus clouds are very high clouds that are domed. They often appear like fish scales. When they appear, it normally means that a warm front is approaching that will cause precipitation over a few days, but not likely any storming. If the clouds are in bands, it is more likely that the precipitation will be heavier. Another indicator of a warm front approaching is a wind from the east. It may take a few days for the warm front to arrive. During the wait the overcast clouds will slowly lower.

Different sorts of fogs exist, but the most common fog occurs when a warm front is nearby. Warm fronts often have small cumulus clouds that are low to the ground and produce rain. If it is cold already and the wind if from the northeast, the rain may freeze.

"Red sky at night, sailor's delight. Red sky at morning, sailor take warning." In mid-latitudes where storms approach from the west, they would obscure a sunset so you wouldn't see red, but a sunrise illuminates tall clouds in the west which means that a cold front is likely coming. Cold fronts are often stormy. Towering cumulus clouds in the west are often visible before thunderstorms. If a cloud has an anvil top, it is more ominous. Cold fronts often pass quickly. Green color in the clouds is from hail.

When there is lightning in the distance, it can come closer in a few minutes, so seek a safe place. Inside a home or car is safe if you aren't touching metal. Avoid hills, roofs, open places or water because you are the tallest there. Next to a tree is safer than elsewhere outdoors, but don't go so close that you are touching it or would be in danger from falling branches. Watch for falling branches in high wind.

Shelf and rotating wall clouds are likely to produce tornados. Seek shelter immediately. Tornados are most likely at the southern end of a group of thunderclouds. The wind may be rapidly changing between different directions. If it is an exceptionally powerful tornado, several of them might be grouped together in one larger vortex. Tornados usually move to the northeast. Tornado season is at peak about the same time that trees become fully leaved.

If a tornado is close, you may feel your ears pop or you may hear it. If you are outside, lay down. Do not hide under things. If you are inside, go into a basement or inner room. Wear a helmet, goggles and gloves if you have them.

Protection

It is random whether you will need protection from people, but everyone needs shelter, so this is a secondary issue. Just being in a locked house does a lot to provide protection. If you are exposed in the environment, you probably have very few possessions with you anyhow that makes you a target. Therefore, there isn't much risk there either.

Mobs don't form over one minute, one hour, or one day. If a major disruption occurs, it is more likely that order will slowly disintegrate, and individuals will act for themselves rather than a mob forming. Therefore, if you need protection, it will be from a single intruder. Most people won't want to risk confrontation. If they know you are home, they won't bother your possessions. Just staying calm and at home is protection. If a mob did form, it would be so rare that you would not likely be the first target, but you would have lots of warning that it is happening.

Most houses can be broken into. Doors can be reinforced with extra support to prevent them being kicked in. However, nothing is completely foolproof. Someone could use a crowbar and sledgehammer to disassemble a wall if they wanted to. Your goal is to just make it difficult. Windows are very easy to break and then enter through. The reason that people don't do that now is that it makes a lot of noise so would draw attention to them. Unless you live in a remote area, don't be concerned with people coming through windows.

Essentials for short term survival

After shelter, water and food are the next needs. Water is the hardest to store in advance. Thin plastic water bottles lose water over time due to osmosis. This is one good reason to have rain barrels. Even if you aren't excited about watering your lawn or garden, just having a barrel can be a lifesaver. Make a list of where you can store water. A tub may slowly leak water out of the drain unless you have a stopper or flap to place over it. Large cans outside often are cracked. In addition, having a bladder to fill with hundreds or thousands of gallons of water might be useful if you think you might have warning that the water system will turn off. Alternatively, if you have access to surface water, instead you should focus on how to purify it with filtration or chemical treatment. See the mid-term survival section for more information on water sources.

Food can be found in most any season and in most any region. However, it is much more effort to find it in the middle of winter or in an arid region. Therefore, it is preferable to have food stocked up to last you through the disaster if it is temporary. One month of food should help you last until either help arrives or until you transition to natural foods. The worst part of winter might last a month or more, but with that much food, it will give yourself time to figure out your plan.

An easy way to stock up food is to buy more of what you already eat. Figure out what you buy in a year and select the items with a long storage life. This is food that you regularly eat anyhow, so just cycle through it to keep it fresh. You wouldn't be wasting any food because you will be eating it. One normal year's stock of dry and canned goods might equal one month of food for you and your family under disaster conditions, depending on how much you eat it. You may need to clear shelf space in your basement. You can save money by stocking your shelves at the next sale. Alternatively, you can buy survival packs of food, but then you are spending money on something that you may never need. If you eat old, expired food, be watchful for botulism symptoms discussed below with food preservation. If you don't have food, see the mid-term and long-term survival instructions below.

If you need medicines for your survival, get what you need ahead. Most medicines are for long-term health, but insulin and some heart medicines are examples of ones that are necessary daily. Refill those medicines as soon as you can and then put it on auto refill, so they keep coming before you need them.

Staying cool in summer is just as important as staying warm in winter. Limit activity in hot times. Stay in the shade. If you have extra water, soak your clothing in it because when the water evaporates, it will cool you. Evaporative cooling works better when the air is dry than when really humid. Mornings may be too humid, but the air dries in the middle of the day. Another way to cool is conductive cooling. The ground and pools of water are usually not as hot as the air, so sitting on the ground or in a pool of water will cool you. Basement floors are the coolest because they are the furthest from the sun. When in the sun, be mindful of any changes in your body. Watch for signs of heat stroke, including dizziness, weakness, or confusion. If you feel different, back off your work unless it is a matter of life and death. Over weeks, your body adjusts to seasonal changes, so slowly add time in the heat or cold each day. The signs of dehydration are similar to heat stroke. Water is best for dehydration. Flavored drinks supposedly for hydration often have sugar which counteracts rehydration. When moderate dehydration occurs, and if someone starts vomiting, don't make them stop heaving, but try to get them to slow the pace. Give water alone for four hours, and then zinc can be given and continued for two weeks. If you have no pills, see below about rice grown in peat or clay. Potassium can also be given, but don't exceed the recommended daily allowance. If you have no pills, see below for dandelions, or try dried parsley.

Mid-Term

Shelter

Security

If you are concerned about your safety in your home, the most likely means of entry is kicking in a door. Doors that open outward are very safe because they can't be kicked in. A single bolt lock may not be sufficient. You could cut a board to prop the door. Either brace it against a wall or nail it to the floor.

The second most likely entry is a basement window. It is very noisy and dangerous for an intruder, so nobody would likely do it while you are at home to protect it. Bullet-proof glass is essentially a sheet of thick plastic. If you have any, it could be held in place with temporary wood framing.

Heat

If you can only heat part of a house, close off other parts of it by tacking up blankets or tarps.

Passive solar

Opening window shades will heat a home. If you have direct light coming through a window all day, it should be enough to keep a house tolerably warm those days except for the deepest part of the winter in northern climates. Close window shades if no direct sun is coming in. You could also pin up sheets over those windows to add insulation.

If the room is getting very warm, you can store heat in heavy materials like brick or water jugs. Have the sun shine on them, and they will release the heat at night. It might be too late to do this if you don't think of it until you have to drag in frozen water jugs.

Fireplaces and wood stoves

Fireplaces are said to have negative efficiency which means that they draw in so much air for combustion, that they cool off the rest of the house more than they heat the room they are in. The heat coming from the fireplace is radiant heat which is infrared light. Warm air is not coming out but going up with the smoke. If fireplaces had an external supply of combustion air, then they would not draw in air to the rest of the house. However, they aren't normally made that way. The negative efficiency assumes that you have another heating system warming the rest of the house, but if you don't then obviously things would get warmer.

Constructing a fireplace at the last minute with limited tools only promotes risk. If the construction is poor, deadly smoke or fire could come into the home.

Wood stoves come in different designs and are still common in historic homes and old European homes. A wood stove is not for appearance like many fireplaces but is a closed system that is often in the middle of a house and built into the house as a bench. They still may draw in cold air if they don't have a direct source.

Bed warmers: Fill a pan with red hot coals, or for safety use stones or sand that has been warmed. Then put the pan between your sheets. It might slide easier if you remove the lid handle. Alternatively, attach a broomstick to a cookie tin.

Lighting a fire: You will be able to find matches or lighters initially. A flint could make a spark or magnifying glass in the sun could start a kindling on fire. However, in the long-term, you might decide to keep one fire burning all night. To make it burn long, use hardwood, and stack it tightly. You need at least 4 inches of wood of solid wood to last eight hours. Partly covering with ash or rocks will slow it more.

Wood supply:

Hard wood, from deciduous (leafing) trees, used as firewood provides more long-burning heat than coniferous (evergreen) wood. The amount of wood stock you need goes up the further you are north. Across the same latitude, the heating need is roughly the same, except there is more need at higher altitudes. A home in Michigan could require 360 cubic feet of wood per 1000 square foot of floor area for one winter to keep a fire. A quarter to a third more or less would be needed for each state north or south of there. Florida and southern Texas are fine with no wood for heating.

Spring before leafing is best for cutting. Autumn, after leaves have fallen, is second best. Cutting wood is labor-intensive. Measure your stove or fireplace and aim for logs that can easily fit in it. Make a workflow pattern. Cut the logs, split with an axe, and then throw them into a wheelbarrow. As with any job, do only a little the first day and slowly do more as you build tolerance. Usually, chopping wood is easier if green. Wood becomes stronger when dried. Exceptions are poplars which become brittle and easy to snap.

Stack wood off the ground so animals don't live in it, and it stays dry. Cover with a tarp or roof to keep it dry. Cut it months before you need it, so it cures or dries.

Don't burn plastics or other flammable materials because most, if not all, emit toxic fumes. Of course, wood does this too, but plastics are much worse.

Kindling is dry grass, paper, or cotton balls. It is what is lit and what gets the tinder burning.

Tinder is twigs. It burns for a while to get the logs burning. Keep your tinder dry.

Solar collectors and greenhouses

Solar collectors are systems designed to collect heat from the sun and store it until needed. Collectors often are placed on the roof of buildings. They are like greenhouses that divert heat into the home using water. Greenhouses can function similarly but just through air circulation. In northern states, solar collectors or greenhouses need to have the same surface area as the sunny side of the roof or up to as big as the whole roof. They'd need to be a quarter to a third larger or smaller for each state north or south of Michigan.

On sunny days, the systems produce too much heat. In the middle of winter, greenhouses without heat storage need to open their windows or else it could damage the plants. Storage of heat is essential for cloudy days. Without storage, a hot system would just radiate the extra heat back outwards. Water and bricks or concrete are good for storage because they have a lot of weight (thermal mass). You want the sun to be focused onto the water in your thermal collector which you pipe into a storage tank. An alternative way in a greenhouse is to have a brick floor or interior wall that the sun directly warms. Large, dark barrels in a greenhouse full of water should also absorb and store a lot of heat.

Starting a system in early fall lets you store up heat that you can use later in the winter. You'd need more storage capacity for this. Heat will be lost through the ground. Try to thermally isolate the foundation. If you are constructing a new greenhouse, before you lay the foundation, put rigid insulation under it and around it. If you are putting the greenhouse on pavement, heat will be lost as it conducts through the material. Breakup the pavement outside of the structure. Above ground, a small bundle of straw can work as insulator.

Geothermal

Geothermal cooling (or heating) normally requires digging deep wells to the water table and then using that water as a source of heating or cooling. Additional supplementation with air-conditioning and heat pumps is often necessary. To dig those wells, install the equipment, and operate it is too much. However, a solar chimney is similar, may be able to be done with less effort, and doesn't require electricity to operate. In the north, solar chimneys likely can cool more easily than heat. Rather than digging deep wells, the source of cool air is tubes buried in the ground shallowly. The ground will stay cooler than the outside air. A long tube would have an inlet away from your home. The hot intake air is cooled by the ground and then comes into your home. To encourage air to flow, a chimney on the sunny side is left open to ventilate air up. When the sun hits the chimney, it warms the air inside and causes convection through your system.

Methane digesters

Methane or natural gas is naturally produced when compost decays away from oxygen. If oxygen is present, then you would only make carbon dioxide. Getting the digestion process going is easy. Any material decomposing in a sealed system will produce methane. Some commercial digesters are available, but it is possible to make one.

The requirements for a digester are first that you have a sealed system that can store the gas produced. This could be a large expanding bag. Second, you need a place for the digestion to occur, such as a bin. Third, you need a way to add compost by the bucketful without adding a significant amount of air. Fourth, you need a tube to draw out the methane to your place of use. Lastly, you need a way to get out the decomposed waste. Alternatively, you could have a batch system for putting in and taking out the compost, but you'd still need methane storage. Even with a continuous system, you would need to clean out the solids every few months. Leave some to seed the next batch.

In most systems you would pour in ground up waste-food particles that have been mixed in water for soupy consistency. Avoid fibrous materials like leaves and branches that are better for the compost pile. After decomposition, the liquid that comes out of the digester is a good fertilizer. Animal and human wastes are good for composting in your methane digester and are a great way to get the process started since they already have a thriving community of microscopic methane producing microorganism.

The digester process needs to develop heat as the microorganism release body heat. Hotter is better. Unfortunately, in the cold winter when you need the most gas for heating, the temperature slows down the organisms. It might take three times as long then. For this reason, this process is more suited to other smaller uses of natural gas such as cooking. Alternatively, make the system three times bigger than otherwise needed. It is not a good idea to have the system indoors for safety reasons.

If you want gas continually, then you must feed the system constantly. Gas might begin to be produced immediately, but you get the maximum out of your compost by leaving it to digest for two weeks. You need storage in the digester, and for the gas. You should have enough gas storage so that it can build up between uses.

To determine the amount of gas you need, you could look on a gas bill. In the US, the unit is CCF or hundred cubic feet of gas. Alternatively, you can convert from wood required to gas equivalent by the ratio of 1 cubic foot of stacked hardwood is about equal to 100 cubic feet of gas. This needs to be qualified that you would get a lot more out of the gas if you find a way to get it into your efficient furnace compared to an inefficient fireplace.

The amount of gas produced depends on the quality of the compost material you are feeding it. Starchy kitchen waste is best. One pound of kitchen waste, not including the mix water, produces about 3 cubic feet of gas over two weeks in summer.

Water

If you are not exposed to the elements, but at home, then water is likely your first concern. If you act immediately, you may be able to salvage much more water than you thought possible.

Drinking requires half a gallon a day which is eighty ounces per person or 10 cups of 8 ounces. Essential washing of hands, face, teeth, and private parts can bring this to two gallons but can be skipped in an emergency.

Water sources

Water heaters: Turn off all valves so there is no seepage back into the system. If you still have gas, turn the thermostat low so that the water isn't heated. The most common size is 40 gallons. Second is 50 gallons.

Toilets: If you haven't flushed them yet, put tape over the handles so no one automatically hits flush, or disconnect the flapper. As long as you don't have a freshener in the tank, you can drink the water without treatment. If there is a freshener, you may have to use it for only cleaning, or construct a char treatment. Most commonly, toilets have 2- or 3-gallon tanks.

Faucets: There may be limited water pressure for a short time. Find as many containers as you can. Fill them with water ASAP and worry about cleaning the water later. This water might not meet drinking water standards without treatment because the water system assumes that high pressure is what keeps out contaminants. If you have time, scrub out garbage cans and then fill them with water. Don't rely on a tub to store water very long because it will likely leak slowly. However, if you are in an emergency, you could fill it and then pan it out as you find containers.

Hoses and plumbing: There may be standing water in garden hoses and in the plumbing. Drain out at a low point.

Humidity: Several options exist for getting a little water from humidity and condensation. 1) Tie a plastic bag over a tree branch in spring or summer. 2) On a sunny day, dig a shallow hole and put a clear plastic sheet over it, and a cup under the low part of the plastic. Hold it down in the middle with a rock. If the ground is not moist, you can put foliage in the hole. You can make a bigger one above ground like a tent. 3) Leave out a towel overnight and wring out the condensed dew or use it for a towel bath. A towel can also soak up dew from the grass.

In many rural areas, it is likely that you have well water at your residence or you have a municipal well nearby. In the short-term, finding a generator to run a pump might be best. To save gas in the generator, you could run it an hour a day. In the long-term, you would need a way to power pumping manually. Some rural water has nitrates in it from fertilizer, but then you are probably already aware of what to do about that.

Rain barrels

The eastern half of the US gets much more water than the western high plateau areas above 2000 feet. Most areas in the East can plan on up to an inch of rain a week throughout the year. Even a small home can provide enough water if you can wait for it.

Trash cans may be best for storing water. They often have the right capacity to match a downspout. A bucket is too small to last a week between significant rainfalls, but if that is all you have, it is better than nothing. A tarp or trash bag can seal cracks in a trash can.

Make sure that the trash can has a flat place to sit. It is worth the time to level the ground with a shovel. Then cut the downspout so that it will come down an inch or so into the trash can. This will help with sealing it later. A hack saw is best for metal and any saw for plastic downspouts. Any tool can be used for cutting if you have the time and strength. Angle the trash can to fit it under the downspout lip as you move it into place. Alternatively, you can reconstruct your downspout with elbows that can be pulled out to easily move the rain barrel.

If you have time, cut the trash can lid so that it snuggly fits around the downspout. Mosquitos love still water and can smell it. To keep them out of a rain barrel, find a way to seal it. A window screen from an abandoned home, carefully stuffed, glued, or stapled into the openings should keep them out. If you have a permanent set-up with valves and hoses, you can caulk around downspout openings to seal them. However, that makes cleaning more difficult.

The volume in a week, if you get 1 inch of rain, is 500 gallons per 1000 square foot of roof area. However, much of that will stay on the roof or immediately evaporate. Plan on collecting at least 80% of it, or 400 gallons which could fill 13 standard 30-gallon trash cans. If you have enough rain barrels, you can chain them together so that they all fill. However, a better strategy is to cover all downspouts with at least one rain barrel.

If you have time, clean out your gutters so that there is less refuse flowing into the barrel. You may have cleaned them yearly beforehand, but it is worth doing it more frequently now.

Roof water needs to be cleaned before drinking but is fine for clothes washing and gardening. See below.

Wells

If you already have a well for your house, hopefully you have a hand powered backup pump.

To determine if open wells are feasible, you need to know two things: 1) Is the ground too hard? and 2) how deep is the water? Around farms, or a community that uses well water, the depth to the water level may be very deep. It could be a hundred feet down to water. Normally, the way to determine water level is to look at the water surface level of rivers and lakes. Water will be higher as further away from the open water because water normally flows in the ground towards the rivers. However, if you live in an area where the groundwater is used as drinking water through wells, then the rivers are recharging the ground water, and the levels are likely lower than the river. However, over years, the water would return to natural levels. Rocky soil may be too hard to dig through without power equipment or weeks of work.

The amount of water produced by the well depends on how porous the soil is. If it is sandier, the water will flow in more quickly.

Closer to a river or lake is an easier place since there will be less digging. However, you don't want your well to flood with polluted river water or surface flow, so further away from the river is better. Water level will fluctuate with season. In the wet season, you might want to dig well below the water level so that you don't have to come back later to dig more when you find you are out of water. This is especially true if the water is coming through the topsoil into the well. You don't want water from topsoil and will have to seal that off such as with a clay plug. Keep wells upstream of toilets, or as far downstream as possible.

Look uphill from your proposed well site to see if any industrial pollutants could have gotten into the ground. Water flows downhill underground too. Former laundromats and dry cleaners were big polluters. If you suspect this sort of pollutant, you may need char treatment which with water treatment. If you know that your area has high arsenic levels, char treatment may be good again, but it is limited. The worst areas of arsenic in the US are in California and Nevada, so they may be too high for char treatment. All US states have regions of higher arsenic. Generally, arsenic levels increase as iron increases in the water so be more cautious if the water looks or tastes like iron. Distillation is an alternate treatment as discussed with water treatment. Also, running water over a rusty piece of steel draws off the arsenic. Several places in Mexico are very high in arsenic, but Canada is not bad. Most chemicals don't build up in plants, called biomagnification, because the chemicals are normally stored in animal fats not plant tissue, so it shouldn't be so bad to put arsenic-tainted water on a garden. Avoid rice farmed in moderate and high arsenic regions. Eating diverse foods helps limits exposure to any toxin. Early symptoms of arsenic poisoning are headaches, confusion, diarrhea and drowsiness. Distinct symptoms that develop later are an increase in white spots on the fingernails and hair loss.

Digging a well you may be able to excavate a hole 5' deep in a day. However, you will want to line it with mortared masonry to prevent cave-ins and keep the water clean. That could slow down the process so that it takes a week to go 5'. Holes over 4' deep must be supported for cave-ins. You want top quality bricks. Even though you could make sundried bricks from the clay you excavate, they would come apart when they get wet or from frost. Kiln dried brick are the best but may be hard to find. Landscaping bricks, or demolished concrete may be a readily available option. Corrugated steel tubes and poured concrete are also options for lining. Keep dark loamy topsoil out of the hole because it is a biological contaminant. When you are done, don't forget about safety, and having an easy way to get the water out. Temporary alternatives to prevent slope collapse are to slope the sides at 45 degrees, or to support the sides with a plywood and wood frame box. However, a hole with 45-degree angle sides requires much more digging. It is about twice the digging for an 8-foot-deep hole. This is temporary because you will have a problem of silt falling in.

Rivers and creeks

To collect water, it may be as easy as dipping a bucket. If the stream is a trickle, you may have to dig into the bed to place a bucket.

River water is a tempting source of water, but there are several cleaning challenges. All river water should be assumed to have biological pollutants. Also, it likely has some amount of industrial pollutant. Avoid rivers with foaming water because of PFAS or go upstream for cleaner water. Rivers may have natural or industrial metals, but this is likely lower than in well water.

Melted snow

Don't eat snow since it will give your mouth painful frost bite. Put the snow in something dark, and put it in the sun, or put in a pan near a fire. Also, you can bring it into a heated space.

Desert and arid areas

Finding water in arid areas is a bigger challenge. Dry creek beds may have water near the surface if you dig there. Look where there is the greenest vegetation. Muddy water from underground is safer than surface water. After digging a hole, use a cup or cloth to get the water. Barrel cacti has water content. Use gloves or burn off the spines. Pull out the plant, and prepare like a pineapple. Eat it to get the water. After a rain, look for puddles in rocks but it will be less clean biologically. The sap of trees can be tapped. See above for trees with edible sap. Alternatives include a solar still and fog nets, but they make take a long time to set up and wait. A fog net will catch water droplets if fogs form. Desert fogs may happen in in coastal deserts. Put the fog nets at high points. A solar still is a clear plastic placed over a humid soil, green vegetation or dirty water. The sun's light heats the humid soil and causes evaporation which collects on the plastic. Make a low point so the water drips into a cup or bucket.

Water Treatment

Some well water may be the only types of water that can be drunk without treatment. Each type of water needs a different treatment depending on what could be in it. Water that is going to be used in cooking doesn't need as much biological treatment. This is also true for laundering water. There is little to do for water with metals in it, but char helps somewhat. There is usually no treatment needed for water used for gardening unless you have very high industrial pollution, or very high natural metals such as arsenic. The soil can naturally degrade many pollutants.

Chlorine Bleach: Will kill biological contaminants. If it is 7-10% chlorine, put 6 drops per gallon and let it sit 30 minutes. Proportionally increase the drops for lower strength bleach. Supposedly, bleach loses strength over time and turns into salt water. If you suspect this, then add more. It is probably not bad as long as it smells bleachy. Bleach is a base. Acids like vinegar can have a similar result. However, tests with vinegar show that you would need to dilute water with common vinegar in a 2 to 1 ratio. Therefore, you'd be drinking nearly pure vinegar.

Solar UV: Will kill biological contaminants. Put a clear plastic water bottle full of water in the sun for a day on a sunny day. The UV will kill anything inside. Filter or settle out dirt and particles so the solar rays can get through the water.

Boiling: Boiling for one minute will kill anything. Some references say longer is needed.

Filtration: A commercial filter with a size of 0.2 microns will remove all biological contaminants. Those are specialty filters, not the ones that some people put on faucets or water pitchers. Clay is a good filtration material. Only use clays that are under the loamy topsoil so that it is not biologically active. A clay filter needs to be A couple feet deep, but use more if the clay is sandy. Pack it in so that the water finds no free channels. Get creative about how to collect the water from the bottom of the treatment column. Never let the system completely dry out or it will crack the soil and open channels. Wood can filter water too. Carve a one-inch long plug the diameter of the tube leading from your water reservoir. . Push the plug into the tube and clamp the tube around it so water doesn't sneak around the edges.

Distillation: Boil the water and collect the steam. This is the ultimate method that will clean anything except a few aromatic chemicals that boil easily like water. Char can deal with residual aroma.

Char/Biochar/Activated Carbon: Charcoal absorbs many industrial chemicals. You know you need this if, after filtering biological organisms, your water still smells. It doesn't work great on metals like arsenic, but still helps. Unless you live in a high arsenic region, it might be enough treatment to reduce arsenic in groundwater to recommended levels. Char does nothing to most biological organisms. Char is essentially ashes. Activated carbon is much more efficient than non-activated. To make activated carbon, you need to make your fire super-hot. You might do that by restricting oxygen by putting it in a closed system with only a couple air holes. The ash should be crushed to a few millimeters in size. The char should then be layered into a column that the water flows through. The char has a life, so check the water to make sure the smell is gone. Don't waste your char on water for laundry.

Food

In rural areas, you are more likely to have access to livestock, and you will find people with knowledge of what care is needed. Since there are fewer homes in rural area, you may have less access to variety of flower garden plants. You would need to switch over to natural foods sooner. Silos of grain may be source of food. Corn pollen is edible.

Avoid collecting food too closely to a road or railroad. Go beyond the bottom of the ditch because any spilled chemicals likely didn't go up the bank on the other side. Avoid areas where the vegetation looks stunted. Lead contamination from historic use of leaded gas is much lower beyond the ditch and gets near to background levels. Railroads often sprayed pesticides containing arsenic, but unlikely sprayed it very far beyond the track bed. If possible avoid the area completely.

Food plan

Eating a variety of foods is good, but these items are best bets to provide for you.

Your body needs to adjust to new foods. The microorganisms in your digestive track are the ones that are best for digesting the food you normally eat. When you change foods you eat, even for modern foods, you might have painful gas. Therefore, with any new food, have a little bit, and then increase it as the new food comes into full season.

The author assumes no liability for any instructions in this book such as eating wild food. If you are not sure if it is safe, don't eat it.

Carbohydrates for energy

Phragmites and cattails: all year except not preferred in summer, and hard to dig in winter.

Dandelion root: all year, but hard to dig in winter.

Chicory root: Fall and maybe winter.

Plantain: seeds collected through summer and fall.

Garden wheat and corn in summer. Pumpkin and potatoes in fall, or as long as will keep into winter. Dried garden starches through winter.

A last resort in winter is tree cambium from certain species.

Protein

Wild meat is an option throughout the year but might be saved for lean times in winter. Meat can be smoked, or salt cured to preserve it. Generally, protein and fats come together. However, wild meat isn't usually a good source of fats, so make sure other sources of fat in other proteins or starches are eaten too. The brain might be the fattiest part of a wild animal.

Spring: Worms in spring might be a last resort if you have nothing stocked up, but they can be found any season. In winter, a worm farm is best. Pollen anthers from pine trees.

Summer: Seeds from maple trees, sunflower seeds, plantain seeds.

Fall: Chestnuts, acorns, walnuts, beechnut, and garden beans. Nuts and fruits in landscaping.

Winter: Dried seeds from summer. Stored nut flower. (You may find nuts still on the ground in winter. I've had walnuts that have stayed out the whole winter.)

Greens

Spring: Plantain and dandelions. Clover, lawn grass, and chicory. Late spring: garden spinach.

Summer: Newest leaves of wild spring greens, or boiled spring greens. Purslane. Garden greens.

Fall: Some garden greens will continue producing, or at least stagnate until you pick them. Set up a greenhouse. Seeds will sprout if soil temperature is above 55 degrees. Cabbage.

Winter: cabbage, kale or greenhouse. Last resort is pine tree needles boiled for tea. Other ideas for greenhouse foods: baby greens are cold hardy, dandelions, sod, plantain, clover, spinach, lettuce, herbs and sprouts of peas, broccoli and beets.

Fruits

Late Spring: Wild strawberries

Summer: Mulberries. Wild berries.

Fall: Grapes, apples, pears.

Winter & early spring: Dried or preserved summer fruit. Maybe sumac berries.

Details

If you are uncertain of a food, you should do a poison check. This works with most poisons but avoid foods in the list below. Your body has a natural reaction against poisons. The way to test for poison is to use that defense in small steps because poisons have differing strengths. Some plants have edible parts, and poisonous parts such as the tomato plant which is from the nightshade family. Therefore, after you have identified the parts that you want to test, test each separately. The first test is to smell it. If it is not appetizing, that is a signal to reconsider the next step. The next several steps can be done all at once, but when doing together, you have to start with fasting for 8 hours. (The reason is that if you throw up, your body might think every food you threw up was also poisonous and make you allergic to it.) The second test is to touch it to your skin and wait 15 minutes for irritation such as stinging, burning, itching, or numbing. Then touch the lip and wait 3 minutes, and then the tongue for 15 minutes. An unusually bitter flavor can mean it is poisonous or at least that it requires leaching. Bitterness is a response that isn't specific to one poison, but many poisons are bitter. That doesn't mean not to eat bitter food, but only if it is extremely bitter and can't be made palatable. Next, swallow a small amount and wait 8 hours. This is the part that requires the preparation against vomiting. Finally, eat a serving of it and wait another 8 hours. A reaction may not mean that the plant is poisonous to all people, because these are the same tests and reactions for allergen testing. Some foods are called toxic because of side effects such being a sedative, intoxicant or laxative, but be careful to observe any changes in your body, and then consider eating at a smaller dose. It is best not to have young women do the poison tests. Their systems are most easily upset because their body protects them powerfully in their prime child-bearing years. If a young woman reacts it may just mean the food was too strong for her. Wild foods tend to be strong. Keep milk thistle seeds on hand when testing foods. Ingesting the seeds reduces organ damage from poisons.

Be very careful that green onions are not death camass because it has a round stem like green onions, but it doesn't have an onion odor. Avoid seeds like apple seeds that taste like almonds because of cyanide. Also avoid wild carrots and anything in a peapod except garden peas. Other known poisonous plants are most lilies, irises/flag, May apple, yew, horse chestnuts, and pokeweed. Some of these like May apple, yew and horse chestnuts might have parts that are edible with the right conditions or processing but aren't worth the risk in most situations.

Common poisons are discussed here. Wild or landscaped almond trees may have bitter nuts. The bitterness comes from cyanide. Boil it with an open lid to remove cyanide. Roasting won't reduce cyanide as thoroughly. Almond trees won't grow where the winters are very cold such as northern great plains and the far NE of the US.

If beans or grains have a strong bitter flavor, that is from lectin which is a mild poison. Anemia is a possible symptom. Cooking through boiling reduces the lectin.

Saponins are soapy residues from plants. See below for using for anti-fungal purposes. Yucca root is an example of a food with saponins. A symptom of saponin consumption is blood problems, diarrhea and vomiting. To remove saponins and the bitter flavor, cook for a long time under low heat.

Alkaloids exist in many roots and other vegetables. It increases in potatoes when they sprout. It will taste bitter but also cause a burning sensation. Symptoms include digestive tract issues. There is no way to reduce it, but it has a higher in concentration in the skins and eyes of potatoes. Alkaloids also exist in mushrooms. Tannin can be a remedy for alkaloid poisoning.

Gingko seeds have various poisons in them. Symptoms include vomiting and convulsions. The poisons are lower in ripe seeds. Some of the poisons such as cyanide are reduced by cooking but other poisons can't be reduced. However, eat only a couple ripe and then cooked seeds a day until you learn your tolerance. Death can occur with as few as a dozen seeds if not properly prepared.

Reed grass (Cattails and Phragmites):
The flower of cattails look like the tail of a cat, brown when ripe in fall, and gray when seeding in spring. They grow about four feet tall. Phragmites plants are invasive from Europe. They are up to nine feet tall and have taken over most marshland in the eastern US. Cattails still grow in standing water. Another reed grass is wild rice. Wild rice is usually in standing water, and produces seed heads not as large as phragmites. Wild rice can be harvested by boat in fall. Lean over the stalk and shake or tap the seeds into a container. Wild rice can be eaten like other reed grasses.

Figure 1. Phragmites

Cattail and phragmites roots are a source of flour year-round but have less starch content in the summer growing season. Look for phragmites plants in areas where there is very low risk of pollution. Only harvest tall plants because some plants 3' tall might have poisonous plants mixed in. Dig the roots but be careful not to mix with other roots nearby that may be from poisonous species of lilies. In standing water, you might be able to pull out cattails if you push away some of the mud first with your boot soles. Solid roots are better than rhizomes, which are stalks below ground. Clean off the roots. Without water, you rub off extra dirt or dry the dirt and shake it off. Wash the roots with a vegetable brush dedicated for outdoor use. Split open the roots. Soaking first might help. In water, rub the white powder and crystals away from the long fibers. Pour the mixture through a screen such as a flour sifter or fine strainer to catch the fibers. Pour through a few times to catch fiber. Try a cheese cloth too. Settle out the flour by letting it sit for a day, and then drain off the water. Either use wet or put in the sun to dry and store in a cool place. The flour has no noticeable flavor.

Stems and rhizomes (underground stems) are more difficult to get out the flour. Consider drying and beating on the ground. For a snack, split open and use fingernail to dig out the white.

The top foot of stems and new budding rhizomes may have tender shoots. Peel down until light green on stem or white on rhizomes. Boil until soft, or peel rhizomes to the inner juicy part and nibble on that. The shoots have a strong green flavor but are not unpalatable.

Cattail flowers can be harvested when still green. Eat like corn on the cob. Pollen is edible.

Bugs and worms:

Generally, bugs are edible with some exceptions. Avoid spiders and do a poison test on bugs with red or brightly colored. Bugs have very good fats and proteins. Fish and birds have good fats because they eat bugs. Crickets and grasshoppers might be caught with butterfly nets, by shining a flashlight on a white sheet at night, or with a fire circle. A fire circle is the start a fire in a large area by simultaneously lighting a fire along all sides. The fire will work towards the center. The bugs will hop to the middle and get cooked there.

You can also make a trap for crickets. Crickets will eat rotting fruit, so use apples that have gone too long. A plastic bottle with a little bait will attract them. Put a few leaves in the bottle so they have a place to hide. Then either bury the bottle so they jump in, or lay it flat and put a ramp up to the entrance.

Hornets and their larva are easiest to collect in fall when they freeze but remove the stinger. Caterpillars are good unless they are too hairy to eat. Ants can be collected by disturbing or digging the nest, shoving in a stick or stem that they latch onto, and then either crushing right away or dunking in water to hold for later. Ants can be eaten raw if they are killed but taste better if heated. Dry frying groups small insects or roasting large ones like marshmallows makes them palatable.

Avoid harvesting earthworms exclusively from areas with no weeds because the area may have been treated with lawn chemicals or excessive fertilizer. If the area has plentiful worms of other types, the pollutants are likely diluted and it won't be as much of a concern. You can find the most worms on wet mornings before the sun is up. If it has rained, they may be on the pavement. If looking on the lawn, quietly and slowly scan a flashlight across the lawn. If you find one, move the flashlight away before it scares it into a hole. Grab the worm near the base of its hole and pull along the ground rather than up. Worms eat topsoil, which is full of biological organisms, so don't eat one unprocessed. Worms are in the ground year-round and can be dug up, but if severed in half it prevents processing. Before eating, clean out the intestinal system of the worm, by leaving them in a sealed bucket with some moist grass. Put the bucket in a cool place. Worms will eat the grass which is edible to people so any residue is not harmful. Then cook the worms and cure them if for storage.

Bugs and worms can be farmed. However, many bugs prefer good food that you would want to eat instead. Worms can be farmed in a compost pile of equal parts leaves and grass. An indoor compost bin can keep them warm and thriving as a food source through winter. They prefer the same temperature that you like, but can remain active down to 50 degrees. They don't need light and are scared of it. Don't cook your compost too hot because they won't like it.

Spring greens:

Lawn greens come out quickly in spring. Grasses (e.g. lawns, corn, bamboo) are edible as greens. The white roots are edible as starch. Singe off root hairs, and then boil, or dry and grind into flour. You could chew the whites and spit out the fiber if it is too much for you. Avoid eating grass from lawns with no weeds because the area may have been treated with lawn chemicals. Lawn chemical stay in the ground at low levels for around a year. Some grass seeds (e.g. wheat, corn, barley, oats, rice) are edible, especially if the seed has no dark lines and no spurs. See "docks" for how to winnow. However, eating the thick part of the roots might be a faster return on labor. Clover, including Dutch white clover buds are edible, but never eat wilted or improperly preserved clover because of mold toxins. Clover might be better boiled.

Figure 2. Dutch white clover

Plantains are common in mowed lawns. The fresh sprouting leaves in spring are tender and bland tasting. The fresh leaves look more spinach shaped than long older leaves. Older leaves can be cooked in salt water to soften. Plantain seeds can be harvested through the summer, dried and ground. They look like small oatmeal. Gather on a windless day by holding over a small container and rubbing.

Figure 3. Plantain

Dandelions have edible greens. They are milder in spring and become bitterer as the season progresses. The plants produce latex, so if someone has a latex allergy, go through the poison/allergy test process with them to see if they are sensitive to it. All of the parts of the dandelion are edible, but I don't know why you would want to eat a milky stem or a white puffball. The roots can get as big as carrots but are likely smaller for plants in mowed lawns. There are several variations of dandelions, and they are all edible unless the leaf if too fuzzy or spiky for your taste. All plants with latex sap can irritate people with latex allergies. Too many leaves may be laxative and increase urine flow.

Meat:

All animals have meat that is edible, but parts of some animals are not edible. Game animals are often very low-fat, so a supplemental fat from oils, seeds, nuts or bugs should be found. Seafood shouldn't be a main source of protein because it is very commonly loaded with metals like mercury. Pollution is especially high in river fish as compared to from the sea.

Catching an animal is often the hardest part, but the concentrated nutrition from it is worth the time. If you have hunting weapons, it will make capture easier than starting from scratch. If you have a weapon, you probably already know how to use it. Trapping will be discussed below.

If you are hunting squirrel and your strategy is to use them as a sustainable food crop, you should harvest in the fall. There is usually a die off in the winter, so in the fall they are the plumpest and the most overpopulated. There are often two litters of young, first in spring, and then in summer, so they can sustain a high cull rate and maintain their population.

Geese like short grass, so mowing and setting up decoys may attract them. Seagulls like short grass, too. You can trap seagulls using a noose with an opening of six inches or so. Hold it open with sticks, and weight the end of the string or tie it down. Alternatively, try bait under a weighted box propped up with a stick, and a string to pull at the right time. Put a little bait at the opening of either trap and put other bait to get them into the area. Seagulls eat everything, including worms. Don't eat the skin of sea birds.

Butchering meat requires a few steps. If it is a land animal, it likely has lots of pests like ticks and mites. Letting the game sit for a while will let its body heat come down and most pests will abandon the carcass. Try letting it sit for half an hour or throwing into a fire for one minute.

Next, you want to butcher it. If the animal has an infection, you could catch it by touching or breathing in its blood, so consider how avoid contact such as wearing gloves and avoiding splatter. You could slit its throat right away so that all the blood comes out away from home. The goal is to remove inedible and toxic internal organs, such as the intestine, first. Hang the animal head down. Cut widely around the anus and genitals then cut the skin from inside to

out as you go up to the neck. Remove the unwanted organs without
puncturing them. Check the liver for spots. If it has spots, discard
the liver and edible organs, too, and make double sure you use
sanitary methods and overcook the meat. Near the liver, find the
gallbladder and remove. The heart, lungs and liver are the parts that
are normally kept. Remove the saved meat from the skin and cook.
Bury all unused parts immediately and wash away blood to prevent
flies from swarming. To smoke meat, hang small strips above a fire
for a day or two until it is dark and brittle. Some smoke houses are
enclosed to keep in the smoke. Green wood (freshly cut) may
produce better smoke but lay it over dry wood or hot coals. Sea
birds have inedible skins, but other bird skins are edible if you want
to pluck them.

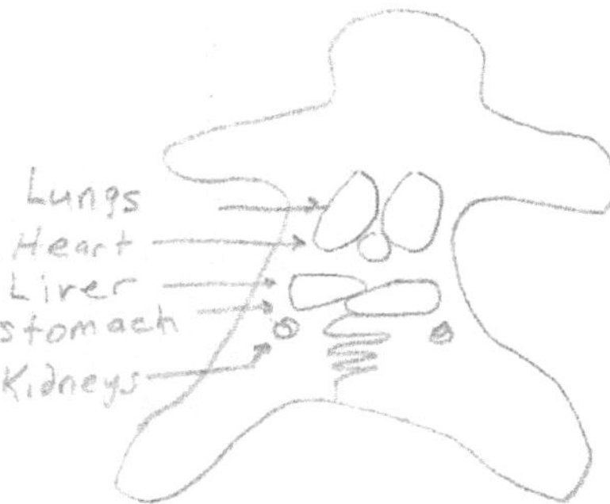

Figure 4. Mammal Body Plan

Trapping:

Squirrels are the most likely source of meat in an urban area.
Therefore, I will focus on the most productive way to trap them. A
squirrel pole can be made easily from common materials and can
catch a couple squirrels a day for each pole if you are lucky. Find
an area where squirrels are active. Find a thick fallen branch about
six feet long and lean it against the tree. The squirrels will run up
and down the branch. You need to make wire nooses to strangle
them. Find wire and tie or nail segments of it to the branch. Make
loops about 2.5 to 3 inches in diameter and point them so the
squirrel's head will go through as it runs up or down the branch.
Their body will catch on the noose and tighten it around their necks.
They will be hanging under the pole when you return.

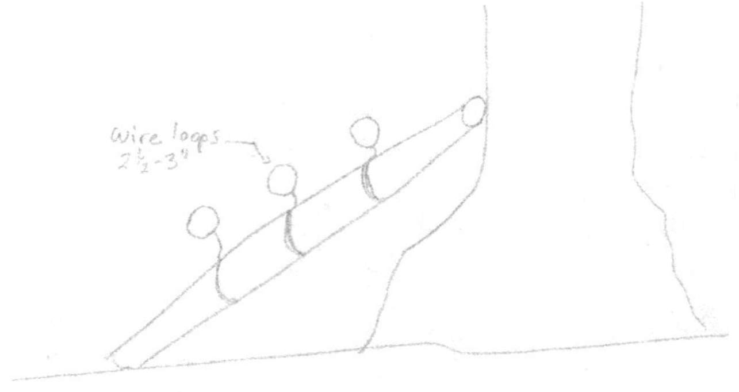

Figure 5. Squirrel Pole

Traps either should have bait to attract an animal or should be in their path. You can also use the noose concept for ground animals. If you see an animal path, you can put the noose in it. Channel the animal to stay on the path with sticks. You would have to guess how big the head is on the animal if you have only seen a path.

Bait for small birds and fish is worms. Bait for squirrels is peanut butter. Rabbits might be attracted to garden vegetables. Baited traps either ensnare the animal or kill it. A rabbit might be content to stay trapped under a laundry basket, but a squirrel would freak out and chew his way out in a minute. An extra-large rat-sized mouse trap with peanut butter would catch squirrels.

To catch small birds, one option is to bait a fishing line with a worm. You would need a small hook. Put the bait on a perch or pole where a bird is likely to want to land. Either wait or tack the line to the perch. Many other types of traps exist for all size and types of animals. Many boil down to the mouse trap concept that when they touch the food, something happens.

A blow dart gun is a very lethal weapon, but probably only short range. You can make it by hollowing out reed grass. You can split it and then bind it closed. Make a dart from a piece of wood. To harden the end, you should fire-treat it.

Trees in spring:

Sap and Manna: Manna is dried sap which is found at cuts in the tree or hidden under the bark. Sap can be collected from acer (maple), birch, hickory, larch, sycamore, and aspen trees. Maple trees are easy to recognize as soon as the maple helicopters/samaras start to bud. Birch trees are easy to recognize because they have distinctive white paper bark that peels off to reveal darker bark underneath. Some sap such as from birch may be slightly irritating. Sycamores also have peeling bark that is relatively smooth and comes off in patches or squares. Older sycamores have the peeling higher on the trunk. The color of bark patches might be brown, tan, white or green depending on the age of tree. To collect sap, pick the largest trees, drill up to three holes of at least a quarter inch diameter for an inch past the bark. A hollow tube or spile will direct the fluid into a bucket. You can make a tube from a young staghorn sumac sprout, and maybe a reed. To make maple syrup you have to evaporate or cook the sap down to one percent of its volume, but you can just drink the sap right away as a mildly sweet drink. Sap collection is best in spring right after a cold snap. At the end of the sap season, the beginning of summer, cork all of the holes with a hardwood (leaf tree) plug.

Maple samaras are the helicopters or whirligigs that fall in late spring. They taste best when picked green off the tree. Peel off the helicopter and eat the soft white seed meat. Dry and store them for winter. Samaras can be eaten brown and for a year afterwards, but they become more bitter with time. If it is unbearably bitter, you can leach out the bitterness as with acorns below. Red maples have reddish brown leaves in spring and small red tipped samaras. Sugar maples have green leaves in spring and larger samaras that are green then brown.

Pine nuts from pinecones are just like maple samaras, but often much smaller and a lot of effort for little yield. The season starts in late spring and varies based on species. Pick unopened pinecones off the tree and dry them by a fire a few hours or until they open. Tap out the samaras, peel off the wings, crack the seed shells in your teeth, and then eat the seed. Avoid black shriveled seeds. You may be able to find the miniature samaras on the ground too under the pine trees.

Pine pollen anthers, or staminate, and shoots can be eaten in mid-spring. Each pine tree species will "bud" at a different time. The new shoots and pollen anthers will appear at the same time, but on alternate twigs. The pollen anther starts light color as it buds, and then grows and darkens. Eat the anther before it darkens, about the time it is full of pollen and ready to release it. You will have about one week when each species is best, so a few weeks total to collect for all species. If you eat after the tips darken, peel off that part so it is not too hard to chew. Put in stews. Eat the fresh shoots as salad after they are long, but before they turn dark green. Only eat the shoots if you are sure that you know the difference between a pine and a yew which produce shoots the same time. Yews are common as landscape bushes and are highly poisonous. Yews are normally short and shaped like a bush. They have waxy dark green needles shaped like short blades of grass.

Gardens:

If you are doing gardening for the first time, plan on getting less food that you would expect. The vegetables will normally be much smaller, less colorful, or odd shaped compared to those selected to be sold in a store. As soon as the vegetable is edible, pick it immediately so that it doesn't rot. If you wait for it to be the perfect size or color, it will rot or go to seed. Kale stays green a long time into the winter if you leave it on the stem. Cabbage is a well-known winter vegetable. It keeps well in cold.

If you have more seeds than you want for planting, you can eat many of them. You can eat pumpkin and watermelon seeds. They are usually roasted before cracking open. However, avoid apple seeds.

Gardens like to have an inch of water or more per week. Measure the rainfall to see how much to supplement.

Decorative plants:

Many flower garden plants are poisonous such as irises, but some have edible parts. The flowers of many decorative garden flowers are edible even if the rest of the plant is toxic, but odds are that you don't have a field of them that can sustain you.

Daylilies have buds that can be eaten if boiled. Daylily flowers are tricky because there is variation among different types, and some may not be edible. Also, eating it might have you develop an allergy to it. All flowers can be laxative. New leaves and buds are less fibrous. Leaves are best younger and cooked. Roots are more likely to be tolerated, and taste best in fall. Young tubers are best, or central part of old ones. Add the chopped root to salad or boil like potatoes. Flower petals can be eaten. The leaves are mildly hallucinogenic, but less so if cooked.

Figure 6. Daylilies.

Garden prickly pear cactus can be eaten. Pick with gloves, burn off the prickly spines, grill and peel, or peel then boil, and then chop as a vegetable.

Yucca flower stalks can be harvested in June before the buds form. They look like big asparagus. Boil and chop. The fruit can be harvested in mid-summer and eaten raw, baked, or dried for winter. If desperate, bake yucca roots a long time in an oven because without that it might cause diarrhea or vomiting. If you haven't eaten all the stalks, collect the red fruit in early fall, and then eat or dry for winter. Instead of picking off the ground in fall, pop open the brown seed pods in late summer before they split.

Figure 7. Yucca.

Ferns, when sprouting and under a foot tall, can be picked and boiled. (April)

Daisy leaves are bitter and tough but can be boiled. Flowers are Chamomile as discussed in medicines.

Figure 8. Daisy (Chamomile).

Dogwood has edible fruit. It is sometime a decorative tree even where it is not native.

Ginkgo Biloba seeds could be eaten raw if necessary. However, it has a mild toxin that has sedative effect, but that is destroyed by cooking.

There are too many species of Hosta list them all. The flowers of all may be edible, but the boiled leaves and stems of only a few varieties are edible.

Wild food in summer:

Summer is peak season for eating off the land. There are lots of available foods. Wet marshy areas are often a first place to look for foods. Leaves, roots, fruit, flowers and seeds are things to try. If you are uncertain about edibility, be sure that you use the poison test methods above.

Berries: Since these are favored foods, odds are that someone will already know which is edible, and which isn't. However, if no one knows, they are worth investigating. Mulberries are easy to find. It is a long tubular berry with many seeds and green stems. Pick when dark. Alternatively, shake branches and collect off of a tarp. When still red or white, it isn't as tasty and may have a mild hallucinogen. Eat the stems and swallow the seeds unless you are having diarrhea from too much fiber. Dry for 2 days in the sun if preserving. Strawberries are in late spring through summer. They are the only berry with seeds on the outside. Elderberries are edible from most elder trees if blue or purple but avoid red ones or cook them.

Common poisonous berries are yew because of the seed, pokeweed which is a tall weed with purple stem and fruits and makes a bad smell when cut, poison ivy, and poison sumac. Most other berries you find are worth checking with the poison test method.

Figure 9. Elderberry Bush

Figure 10. Pokeweed

Pollen from Bulrush, Cattails, and corn is edible. Mix in flour.

Docks and sorrels are common edible plants. (Curled/sour dock, burdock, sheep sorrel) They are tall leafy green weeds. Great Burdock is also called Elephant Ears in the U.S. Some you can eat raw in summer, but some must be boiled because of toughness and

for taste. The plants are tougher but still edible through winter.
Seeds are also edible. To harvest docks and sorrels, first, thresh
seeds loose from chaff by beating them on the ground with a flail,
which is like long nun-chucks. Alternatively, beat a bundle against
the ground. Second, winnow in the wind to blow off the lighter
chaff from seed. Roots of burdock are edible if boiled. Leaves,
stems and roots are better off of young plants.

Figure 11. Curly Dock with green seeds

Goat's beard looks like a mammoth dandelion puffball when going
to seed. The root is edible but cook it to make it tender.

Nuts:

Walnuts are easiest to pick up in mowed grass. After the peel
softens and darkens, you might find that stomping on it is one way
to get the peel off the shell. The peel will discolor your skin if you
touch it. Crack the nut with nutcracker or hammer. Pick out the
nutmeats with a nutpick or jewelers screwdrivers. Store in a cool,
dry place for longer shelf life.

Figure 12. Walnuts

Beechnuts rain down in fall. Tarps, pavement, or mowed grass would help collect them as they fall. Mowing or burning would get rid of ground clutter. Limit beechnuts to occasional use because they are one of the plants with higher defense mechanisms. Eating too many can irritate the small intestine. Beech trees are easy to recognize. They have smooth grey bark. Kids find this tree the best for carving initials into.

Figure 13. Beechnuts

Chestnuts and white oak acorns are edible raw, but you might like them roasted. You will have to fight the squirrels if you want any because they prefer them and go for them right when dropped. See the figure for difference between white and red oak, but there are local variations. You can tell for sure what type it is by chewing a small sliver but be prepared to spit. Acorns from red oak trees are intolerably bitter but can be eaten if the bitterness is leached out (see below). Oaks and similar trees have lots of pests in the form of tiny worms (weevils) that eat the nuts. To kill the weevils, in spring carefully set ground fires to burn up all the refuse on the ground. Keep the grass low, or mow or burn it so you can find nuts as they fall in late summer and autumn.

Figure 14. Red and White Oak

Nut trees often go through alternating years of heavier and lesser production. For example, after a drought year, the next year they might double production.

Squirrels prioritize acorns second after chestnuts and often there are many acorns left after the squirrels have picked them. If you have a pest problem, you will be able to see holes bored through the shells, and the nut may feel hollow. Oak trees are easy to locate. In spring and summer, look for large squirrel populations. In fall, look for acorns, and it winter, look for the only tree that still has many leaves on it. Sun-dry the shelled acorns if you are not going to process them. They should be fine for a while if no weevils are eating them in your larder. If you find any weevils, they are edible. To leach the acorns, soak in a flowing stream for one day, or boil them with changes of water. Crushed acorn powder will leach more quickly. Taste and repeat until the bitterness is acceptable. Dry the flour and save for winter.

Horse chestnuts can be edible. You have to leach the horse chestnuts like acorns or else they are poisonous.

Locust tree seeds are commonly used as the flavoring carob. The seeds of the black and honey locusts are edible if cooked. Like most pods, they are poisonous, but the poison is destroyed in cooking. May have to drain water. Additionally, the pulp of the honey locust pod can be eaten directly and is sweet like honey. The pods ripen in autumn but may need to be picked since they may not fall until spring. Black locusts are native to the Appalachian and Ozark Mountains but have been planted as décor. Honey locusts are more widely distributed in the east. One way to distinguish the honey locust is by the pod that is more reddish versus the black locust pod is black.

Fall fruits:

Apples, pears and grapes can be harvested. Wild grapes are small, seeded and taste horribly bitter if you harvest too late. If harvested earlier they may be only tart and can be mixed with other fruit. When they change color, put several in your mouth and roll around with your tongue. After the juice has been sucked out, spit out the seeds. The grapes are often covered in white powder called bloom which aids in fermenting to wine. From my experience, the ones with white powder need to be harvested immediately when changing color because they appear to dry faster. Some gardeners have cultivated vines. Look for characteristic grape leaf.

Rose bushes produce edible small fruits. Most fruits such as plums, apples, cherries peaches and pears are in the rose family. If you see a tree that is shaped like a fruit tree, has the typical leaf shape, and has small fruits, it is likely a type of a rose. Most fruits from these trees and bushes are edible with care. Seeds contain cyanide, but likely not fatal unless many are eaten. Bitter fruits may be less so if picked after the first frost, frozen, or when boiled before eating. The early signs of excessive cyanide are trouble breathing, weakness, headaches, dizziness, so be on the lookout for those when eating bitter fruit. Sour, hard fruits soften with boiling. Cherry inedibility is related to bitterness caused by poisonous cyanide. After removing seeds, boil the fruit. Try various ways to reduce the bitterness. Plant seeds fall through spring. They produce fruit usually in about six years. After twenty years, you may need to chop them out and replant them.

Pear varieties vary based on species. Some pears ripen only after being picked, and others ripen only on the tree. Try it out to see which you have.

You may have to fight off or smoke away bees from the apple trees. Bees will cut into the ripe apple to get sugary juice, but those apples are still edible.

If you have a lot of apples but need winter food, consider making cider. The apples need to be crushed and pressed. Fermentation will happen with native yeasts, but if you have commercial yeast, it can be used for more reliable flavor. Apple fermentation to cider happens best at cool temperatures and with a filter cover. The cool temperatures slow the process and preserve desired flavors. Avoid plastic containers if possible. A bad smell doesn't necessarily mean that the cider will turn out bad. After completion of fermenting, seal in bottles to limit access of undesired contaminants or other native yeasts that might turn it into vinegar. If you want vinegar, submerge chunks of apple in water and then wait 2 weeks, strain and wait another 4 weeks. Botulism is possible in food stored without preservative. Keep foods as cold as possible to inhibit its growth. The more acidic the food, the more natural resistance it has to botulism and cider is acidic. Symptoms of botulism are tiredness of facial muscles spreading to upper body. Pressure cooking foods is the only way to be sure that the bacteria have been killed in preserved foods but isn't needed for cider.

Crab apples are apples that are at most two inches in size, but often much smaller. Use only after seeds have turned brown. They are tart and are best boiled after deseeding. Good for pectin. Identification: Cut fruit to confirm it has five seed cases in a star shape. (Rarely the number varies from five.) Each case likely has two seeds. Leaves are oval with small serrations. It is tempting to eat the seeds because they may be very small, but they contain cyanide.

Cambium:

Cambium is the white inner bark of a tree. You are killing the trees by harvesting the cambium, so keep that in mind.

Tree cambium can be harvested any time of the year. You can harvest it in winter, but a better choice is to harvest cambium in spring when chopping wood and then dry and grind it for winter. Store in a sealed container.

To prepare cambium for consumption, boil it three times for half an hour each, changing the water each time. It should be pink and tender, and compatible with stew recipes or as a noodle alternative.

Species of tree that have edible cambium are fir, acer (including maples), alder, birch, beech, ash, larch, mulberry, spruce, pine, cottonwood, poplar, aspen, willow, hemlock, and elm. The cambium has more tannin than in nuts, so you might taste it.

Sumac:

Poison sumac has white berries. Staghorn sumac and other good ones have red berries that are tan under the skin. Even though staghorn is not poisonous, as with most foods poison is a level of degree. It is related to poison sumac. Don't base a diet off sumac. Chew seeds, or crush, boil and drink the tea. There are many types of sumacs, and they provide very little benefit except a little vitamin C, so sumacs should not be a first choice to avoid the danger of poison.

Pine tea:

In winter, any pine needles can be boiled for vitamin tea. In summer, it is easier to eat the freshest needles.

Salt, preservation and minerals:

If you are on the sea, you can evaporate water in shallow trays or boil it. If you are landlocked, you can get it by boiling hickory roots until only the scale is left in the pot. Freshwater has some salt and deposits it on sand, so running water through the sand extracts salt which can be boiled down. Alternatively, some animals eat the ground for salt, but it is difficult to figure out what dirt has rock salt *and* is safe to eat. Tasting is the best judge if it contains salt. It could always be boiled first for safety. Look for something looking like rock salt in flat areas that may have been formerly a lake or seabed. Halite is a sediment that forms in areas that were once seas. Geologic uplift may expose layers of salt. Salt looks like crystals, but of any color, but often white or clear. Dandelion leaves are high in potassium salt but relying solely on that may make your potassium levels too high causing heart palpitations. Freshwater has only one percent of the salt of seawater, so you'd have to evaporate one hundred times as much water. Groundwater usually is more salty than freshwater. It might be easier to trade for salt with people on the sea.

Related to salt is iodine which is need to ensure thyroid health. Under normal conditions, commercial salt is iodized. Rock salt usually has no iodine. If you run out of iodized salt, you would need to eat seafood or kelp to get iodine. Less than a gram of dry kelp is required per day. Landlocked people would have more trouble obtaining iodine. Often meats, freshwater fish and animal products such as milk and eggs have some iodine, but not much. Nuts, mushrooms and sometimes cereals (grains) such as rice have it if grown in the right soil. The animals and cereals get their iodine from the ground. Iodine is lowest in sandy soil and the highest in clay, especially if it is swelling (increasing volume when adding water). Since clay has the highest iodine, grow your cereal crops there, or have your food animals graze there. Loam or peat has iodine, but the plants can't extract it from the soil. However, see other discussions related to arsenic about avoiding eating too many cereal crops. See further discussions of iodine under long-term health. For landlocked people, trading for dried kelp is probably the number one priority. Iodized salt might be available if some people have high technology still. Medicinal potassium iodine may be consumed despite warnings on the bottle, if diluted properly. When used for dietary purposes, it must be diluted below a concentration of 2%. Proper dosing is important because a large dose can be fatal. Symptoms of overdose start to appear at eight times the normal dose for men. For men, the ideal dose of iodine is 150 micrograms or 0.15 mg per day which is half of an average-sized, 3 mm diameter sphere, drop of 2% iodine. Women need twice as much. Children require slightly less than men. Freshwater has roughly the same proportion of iodine to salt as in seawater, so if you use freshwater to provide salt, you are getting iodine too.

Minerals can be found in the soil. Clay can be a source of minerals in the diet. However, mineral content varies by soil type. Soil can be a source of vitamin B-12 but boiling to kill microorganisms might dissolve the B-12. Another warning is that lead and zinc levels can be high in soil. By eating a wide variety of foods throughout the year and getting salt from water, you should get enough minerals. Minerals are absorbed by plants and then are in animals because they ate plants. Aim for eating grains, legumes/beans, seeds, vegetables, leafy greens. Also consider eggs, dairy and meat including red and fish. Anemia and goiter are symptoms of low minerals, so pay attention to pale skin and swollen necks or thyroids. Vitamin C is found in acidic fruits and helps absorb minerals. Vitamin deficiency can result in beriberi, scurvy, pellagra, and rickets. Generally, be aware of any sign of weakness that could be from vitamin deficiency. Sandy soils are deficient in zinc, so grow foods in a variety of soils. See later for more information about vitamins and minerals.

Preserving vegetables: Kimchi can be made from cabbage and other vegetables like carrots. For each pound of thinly sliced cabbage, onions and carrots add one half teaspoon of salt and mix. After 15 minutes, press cabbage until there is enough liquid to cover the vegetables. You can add apple, ginger, chili or garlic or all. Place in jars and be sure it is well covered in its own liquid. Leave a gap at the top of the jar for carbon dioxide to collect, then close the jar. Open every several hours to let out the carbon dioxide and recheck that the vegetables are submerged. After a few days when it is well fermented find a cool place to put the kimchi so that the fermentation process slows.

Other vegetables can be pickled. First remove the water by soaking in salt brine for 24 hours. Brine should be five percent salt by volume. Next make a vinegar solution that is two parts vinegar to one part water and one percent salt. Blanch (briefly boil) the vegetables in the vinegar solution. Then fill a jar leaving room at the top. Add the vinegar solution to the jars, re-boiling it first if not still hot. Try adding different spices at different times in the process to see what you like. When sealing jars try turning upside down for a few minutes to get them hot.

Jarred fruits need a tight lid or covering like wax or food oils. Wax can be made like hard candy. Use 1 cup sugar, up to one-quarter cup water and an acid like vinegar. Boil until thick. If you are making your own sugar from boiling down filtered juices, you can stop when it is a thicker syrup but not yet crystalized, and then add no water. Tree sap that is edible, like maple, can be boiled to make a waxy syrup. Pine rosin can be used even though it is not generally considered edible. Beeswax and rosin can be mixed. Wax can also be made by putting a little vinegar into warm milk, but it may be too hard and granular to use to seal food jars. Foods preserved under wax or oil are less safe from botulism than those that have been pressure cooked and put in sealed jars. Therefore, it is more important in this case to either use only acidic foods or to add acid to it so that it slightly pickles. That is why vegetables, which are often low acid, are commonly pickled.

Oils can be made by processing the source. For corn oil, crush the corn, then put it into a press. The liquid that runs off has oil floating at the top. There may be food particles floating, too, that need to be screened off. Also, there may be some water in the oil, so set it out to evaporate the water, but cover it with a screen.

Cooking

Meat should be cooked to 165 degrees. The color and texture will change when done, so you will probably be able to judge it. Warnings about not relying on color may have to do with aged or old meat browning before it is cooked. If in doubt, heat the meat until it sizzles, which is well above the minimum temperature.

Hobo (or camp) stove: Take a large can such as cookie can, coffee can, or large can of beans. Use a bottle opener or other tools to make a large hole near the bottom for feeding in twigs. Put several vents around the bottom and a few at the top. Run wires across the top if your pot will need it. Start the fire with kindling such as dry grass. Feed twigs in to keep it going at desired flame. Don't burn manufactured items like plastics because of the toxic fumes.

Wood stove or camp burners: You likely know how to use them if you have them.

Solar ovens: A solar oven is like a miniature greenhouse, but with extra light reflected in on the food. On a sunny day, you can cook anything. The sun can be focused onto food which raises the temperature very high. The amount of heat you get is directly related to how much sun you focus onto the oven. You can use foil or mirrors to reflect light. You can cook in minutes if you have a good design, but likely you should plan on using three times longer than normal for baking, so foods that take an hour could take three. A dark pot will absorb the light better. A trick to cut the time is to put only minimal water in. Water takes a lot of energy to heat up. Therefore, solar cooking is not recommended for stews or root vegetables. You can put the solar oven on a hot surface like pavement or car hood to draw in all of that heat.

Open fire: This is better than a hobo stove or solar oven if you have anything that needs to cook a long time like baked potatoes, or large pots of stew. Baked potatoes are good wrapped in foil and thrown into the hot coals until soft. A ring of stones or garden bricks provide some safety and also reflect the heat up on to the food. An oven rack placed on the bricks can support pots. Open grilling of meat should be at higher levels out of the flame. Softwood from coniferous or needle trees burns faster and easier but is likely to spark. A charcoal grill is good for a small fire.

Ovens come in many designs. They can be inside as part of a heating source or separate in a summer kitchen. Ovens can be brick or stone that is stacked, or ovens can be clay. The oven heat from its first use would fire or harden the clay. The heat source is often softwoods that have been dried for six months to reduce smoke production. The food might be placed in the flame or on a layer above that is separated by stone or clay. Flatbreads are made by putting the unleavened dough onto the hot surface. An oven might be a clay or metal Dutch oven that is put on an open fire. A beehive oven is a large dome shaped oven which is heated for hours, and then used for cooking bread when hottest, then biscuits or custards when still moderately hot, and finally used for drying food when warm.

Pressure cookers cook quickly because they seal the liquid which keeps it from boiling. When liquids boil, they lose much heat through steam. Pressure cookers require precise construction so that it has an appropriate valve for release. It is ideal for cooking meat and hard foods since they take a long time to cook otherwise. Beans may froth, so only fill at most half full.

Health

Washing

Washing the hands and face are important to keep from infecting yourself with organisms on things you have touched. Washing private areas is important to avoid rashes. If going barefoot, washing feet becomes important. No other part of the body requires washing. Washing the rest of the body is a modern invention that helps in urban areas where people need to be sociable but is not necessary unless there are cuts and scrapes on the skin. It was more likely in the past to use perfumes to mask scent than to wash it away. This changed relatively recently with running water.

Sanitizer and rubbing alcohol are good for sanitizing hands. Sanitizer does not clean, but only kills biological organisms. Pine tree tar can be removed with cooking oils.

Rubbing with a mixture of ash and sand might be a substitute for a wet washing.

If you want to give yourself a field bath, dew on a towel left out for the night might be good enough. If you end up with surplus water, you can make a camp shower. Take a dark trash bag and cut off the tip, and then clamp it so you can control water flow. Fill it with water and tie it off. Place in the sun to warm the water. Alternatively, leave a hose full of water in the sun and control water with a spray nozzle. Drape the water container over your shower head, or from a tree branch. When showering, don't let the water run, but wet the body, soap, then rinse. A luxury would be to fill a bathtub with water heated on a fire. A few people may be able to use the water before it is too disgusting.

Dishes

Run the dishes through clean sand. Alternatively, just wipe away food particles. Wash dishes too much can make people less healthy because eating fermented food is beneficial for the health. Rot is good.

Toileting

If you have river water, and a reliable system to take away the waste, you could still use toilets by filling the tank each time with a few buckets full of water.

Men and women can urinate outside with no consequences except loss of privacy. A bush or shower curtain might provide enough privacy. Urine makes a great fertilizer, but is too strong, so dilute it in four or more parts water.

For the short term, place a garbage bag into the toilet for solid waste. A better plan is to save this for bad weather when you don't want to go outside. It is your discretion about whether to dispose the bag after every use. If you bury the waste, your goal is 18", but that is mostly so animals aren't attracted to it, so less is sufficient unless you develop an animal problem. Keep away from gardens and water supplies. After a year or more in the ground, or a month in a hot active compost pile, the waste can be used as fertilizer. See instructions below.

A next level solution for toileting is to dig a shallow trench. Squat over and then cover with shoveled dirt progressively.

An outhouse is the long-term solution. Keep away from well water. Place the outhouse downwind. Prevailing winds in upper latitudes are from west to east. In the tropics, the prevailing winds are east to west. Place an outhouse as far downwind as possible, but then convenience is lost if it is far away. Construct the outhouse set so that the seat and lid fit tightly. That will keep in smells and keep out flies. The pit depth is your discretion. The sides normally don't need support/shoring if you go only 4'. You can move the outhouse as needed if you build it on skids or wheels and have enough strength to pull it. Old outhouses were solid wood, but that was because of what they had available. It only needs a seat, but it's nice to have privacy and a roof. Shower curtains or tarps could provide both functions.

Laundry

Most clothing can be worn until people complain of the smell. Hanging in the sun and wind does two things. First, the wind blows off odors. Second, the sun's UV rays kill any germs. Brushing off dirt might be sufficient, but as a last resort it could be washed.

Underclothing that is soiled should be washed. In a five-gallon bucket, put a few gallons of water and soap. Use a toilet plunger to plunge the clothing. After the first use, the plunger will be clean too. Wring out the clothing and hang up to dry. Soapy water should be thrown away. Soap can be made by leaching lye from wood or ashes, warming it and then adding it to oils. See instructions in long-term health.

Sun exposure

Wear sunblock in the early season until your skin adjust to the sun. Layers of clothing protect from the sun, too. Knit clothing lets through sun. To build up tolerance of the sun, start with thicker knit clothes and work towards thinner. See other ideas under long-term health.

Trauma and burns

See also the section under major trauma for more details.. Aloe helps work on minor burns.

Willow bark can be made into aspirin. Chew on the bark. See precautions below.

General first aid is ABCD: Airway, Breathing, Circulation, Deadly bleeding.

One way to stop bleeding and seal an open wound is to cauterize it. A metal item such as a knife is heated, then applied to the wound. It causes the blood to coagulate instantly forming a scab. The goal is not to do much damage to the skin.

Pests

Ticks

Avoid walking through grass or thick brush because ticks wait there to grab on. Wear light clothing so you or your partners can see ticks. Inspect your skin, especially hairy areas within one day. Pinch the head and pull to remove it. Throw it in a fire or step on it, but don't pop it because blood will shoot everywhere.

Lice

The fastest way to rid yourself of head lice is the shave your head. Alternatives are to make a comb with extremely fine gaps. Wash the comb after use. Repeat combing after seven days to get the next generation. See topical anti-parasitic in the section on skin.

Body lice live in clothing, so inspect clothes and bedding of infected people and severely wash or burn. Body lice are 3 mm long and have a red backend. If fever develops, check for typhus. Otherwise, use steroids and antibiotics.

Roundworm and other worms

It is best to drink clean water to avoid roundworms and other worms. Most realistic treatments require medical help. Garlic tea for two weeks might help. If they grow on the skin, removal with a knife might work.

Chiggers

Chiggers are mites that are half a millimeter wide. They feed off of animal skin. To control, keep animals and pests away. Most squirrels are infested with them. Exposure most often occurs when sleeping outside in an area where animals are common. They don't easily propagate indoors. If needed, use an antihistamine if you have some to relieve itch until symptoms are gone. Also see Skin for anti-itch.

Scabies

Infestation of scabies may look like rashes or pimples. They are very itchy. Looking closely, you may be able to see burrows in the skin. It is likely to find them on the hands, in the groin and other protected joint areas. On very old people it may spread over the whole body except the face and crust over. It takes skin to skin contact with an infected person to transfer the mite, but recently used clothing or bedding should be avoided by others. Avoid contact with animals looking mangy. Treat with antihistamine, and anti-itch cream. Topical insecticides are used to kill the mites, but if you have access to sulfur, use a 10% solution in oil. See topical anti-parasite in the section on Skin. The alternative is dig them out. Scratching is an appropriate response. To perform minor surgery, have rubbing alcohol, prick the skin, and rub with the alcohol. A pimple means the mite babies are ready to burst out.

Bed bugs

Beg bugs are expected to be a major threat. They were prevalent in previous times. Bed bugs normally only come out of hiding spots at night. Beg bugs are 1 to 7 mm in size. They are brown and oval with a segmented shell. If bitten, you would see many bites clustered or in a line on skin, leaving blisters. Bedbug bites are not a health concern, except that they may increase your level of inflammation. Mostly they are a quality-of-life issue. Infestation comes with other people through their clothing or possessions, so inspect all guests for patterns of rashes before they enter your home. The solution for keeping bedbugs out is to seal all crevices like electrical outlets and wash all clothes and bedding. To get rid of them, you need to burn everything in the home. Wash all pets. Sanitizing clothes and possessions in a solar oven to 131 degrees should kill them. Alternatively, you could freeze them below negative 20 degrees for a few hours. Fumigation by burning peat may work but then nobody will be able to stand the smell afterwards. If you can stand the smell of tobacco, try that instead to fumigate. Heated natural turpentine oil may be an acceptable incense. Also, try cannabis as fumigant, or under mattress. Without insecticides, it may be easier to walk away from a home for three months. There are many home remedies to try to drive away bed bugs. Try and see if they work for you.: Black walnut leaves either rubbed on the skin or placed nearby; black pepper spread over or under bed; crushed mint leaves over or under bed; geranium; or smoke tobacco. Smoking tobacco isn't recommended but if it comes down to bed bugs or cancer, you need to make a choice. It is the addictive nicotine in tobacco that seems to be the effective drug against bedbugs. However, fumigation with it or using as incense may be sufficient. Centipedes might prey on bedbugs. Centipedes have painful bites, so you may not want them crawling around, but if the choice is between centipedes and bedbugs, you might compromise.

Leeches

It is possible for a leech to transfer disease, but it is extremely unlikely. Avoid polluted water that they favor. Allergic reaction is possible. Bandage the wound if it bleeds. All leech foot injuries should be handled more seriously than other locations because of closeness to ground infections.

Bees and wasps

Bees normally won't bother someone unless they are near the hive or step on them. Wear shoes in clover patches. Keep beehives out of area where people will work or play.

Wasps will sting someone with very little provocation. Wasps prefer to put nests in any place with protection but will build on tree branches if nothing better is available. Therefore, seal any areas that could provide protection. Bird houses that aren't occupied by summer should be closed so wasps don't use them. If a wasp nest is going to be hazardous because of closeness to activity, you may want to remove it. Wasps are less active in cold and in the middle of the night. Wear a bee keeping suit if you have one. First, slowly and quietly approach. Second, wrap a trash bag around the nest. Third, pull the nest free and gently put in the bag. Lastly, seal the bag and either crush the contents, put in a hard-sealed container, or take far away. Alternatively, a wasp nest can be smoked out to make the wasps abandon it, but don't burn it.

Long-Term and Miscellaneous Issues

In the long-term, such as over years, a variety of foods, crafts, or trades need to be developed. Some of these instructions are for planning rather than something you can act on right away. For example, complete instructions on how to smelter metal isn't given. However, with this gives you a the information to think about what are reasonable goal over long-term.

Health

Causes and solutions to health problems are discussed. Modern health problems like Type 2 diabetes, high blood pressure, and problems related to pollution except for smoke, are not expected to be prevalent in these situations in the long-term. Cancer is primarily caused by modern lifestyles and pollution. Therefore, these health problems won't be discussed as health concerns. Lifestyle diseases normally improve with time when adopting healthy lifestyles, but there are exceptions such as cancer. If you have medicines for current health conditions, they lose strength with time. The rate of loss often depends on temperature of storage. You can try old medicine if that is all you have but start with a normal dose and work up gradually. Most medicines have side effects. When you reach your normal level of side effects, that is a good indicator you are at the right dose of weakened older medication. Follow the recommendations for medication storage to preserve their potency.

General health

Meditation is helpful for mental and physical health. There are many ways to meditate including through prayer, yoga or tai chi. Meditation is focusing the mind, not sleeping. Each person can choose a focus that works for them. Closing eyes is recommended, but not essential. Most effective is to focus on hearing and feeling slow, rhythmic breathing. For reduction of tension headaches, focus on slackening the muscles on the head such as around the mouth. To learn to focus on specific body parts, focusing on a low dull pain may be helpful. Otherwise, start by focusing on your hands to see if you can make them hot just by thinking about them. Exercises using balance fit well with meditation because balance requires clarity. Once you have mastered control of focus on the body, other benefits are open to you. For pain management, if the pain is relatively constant, focusing on the pain can make it go away. If the pain is sporadic and jabbing, focusing on other pain may be helpful, even pain that is self-inflicted by pinching yourself. For aiding sleep, you can slowly scan your body from feet to head and back. If you can repeat this slowly a few times, then you realize you've been asleep. Other methods of scanning include the tai chi flow and yoga oam. In the yoga oam (pronounced o-ah-mm), your focus flows from down from mouth, to chest, towards your belly. For deepest serenity, focusing on the belly below the navel is recommended. Optional items include posture, mantra or saying, and objects such as prayer beads. For religious meditation, focus on your perceptions. You may be able to change your visual perception of an object by focusing on it.

Muscles and joints: If you injure muscles or joints, then they will normally repair with effort. However, severe joint wear is permanent. Your goal should be to prevent permanent injury by having strength and flexibility. Strength will reduce wear by lowering the demand on the joint. All muscles should be stretched for flexibility and to open inflamed joints. Stretches shouldn't be to the point of pain because that can inflame the joint. Don't stretch past what would be a normal limit on motion because it can hyperextend the joint. To increase flexibility, move each joint forward and back, using external force if necessary. If you are doing hard labor with specific joint motions during the day, come up with stretches that open those joints. To open tight or injured joints, do many stretches on the joint daily, and then after healing, continue a normal exercise plan. If your joints are still painful, then try eating onion which is anti-inflammatory. Also, try soup from peony roots and sap resins from poplars and cottonwoods.

There are dozens of major muscle groups. Those don't include minor muscles such as those in hands, feet and toes, and internal muscles like the heart. Working the major muscles gives a basic level of strength, but you may still find that you are lacking in other ways. Many strength-building exercises can use your own body weight. Most yoga positions are modern inventions, and so you could invent your own poses by locating major muscles and then trying different poses until that muscle bears your weight. Otherwise, find a book with photos. A yoga sun salutation is a typical exercise sequence that covers many muscle groups. Hold each position and move smoothly between them. When working on flexibility, hold a stretch for more than 6 seconds such as 15 to 30 seconds because muscles stretch with time. For the first 6 seconds, the tendons resist stretching. Start standing, squat with arms raised, bend forward and down as far as possible, hold legs, and then arch back, go to a push up position, then arch back as you look up, move into downward dog, which is making an upside-down V-shape with your body, stand with one leg forward while bending that leg at ninety degree and arms raised. Next, go back to the push up and repeat all steps until the other leg is forward. Then do the first steps again in reverse order until standing erect again. Repeat as many times as necessary. The sun salutation misses some abdominal muscles, twists, side stretches, and arm, hand, and toe muscles. For abdominal, lay on the back and lift legs and back to form a V-position. For this, higher is a lesser work out than lower. Twists are best done sitting so you can get leverage to twist by pushing on the ground or raised knees. For side stretches, use standing positions where you bend sideways with one leg out, and reaching up and down. You may modify any exercise to increase or decrease it so that it is adjusted to your ability. An example of an adjustment is to go higher or lower in a squat. To make the exercises into a fuller yoga, include meditation and breathing.

Arthritis is any inflammation of joints for any reason. However, some causes of it can be avoided by taking care of joints and muscles as discussed above. Still, repetitive activity can wear down joints. Do a variety of work tasks rather than the same thing over and again. If you get tired or feel strained, and you can return another time, then switch to another task. If in pain, try topical pain management first.

Hypothyroidism: The most common cause of hypothyroidism before modern health systems was lack of iodine. See in iodine in the section about food plans. Symptoms are tiredness, slow heart rate, constipation, and weight gain. Also, the front of the neck could be swollen. There are no easy solutions for this type of problem except getting more iodine.

For preventing underarm odor, scrubbing helps. Also, if you have mineral salt, rub a block of it under the arms.

Major trauma

See ABCD above. (Airway, Breathing, Circulation, Deadly bleeding.)

To sanitize instruments, boiling kills germs instantly. Lower temperature water of 160 degrees can also kill quickly, but you would have to measure the water temperature.

Gauze, bandage: Try cattail fluff. Large leaves of non-poisonous plants can wrap a wound but check if absorbent. Charcoal ground and sprinkled on cut will stop bleeding and act as an antiseptic. You can crush or grind up goldenrod leaves and put on as a poultice. Goldenrod is a tall weed with tiny yellow flowers. Some people suggest moss for a bandage, but most of the time moss will cause infections so only use in an absolute emergency to stop blood flow. Grow a small patch of each bandage source you will use so it is always ready.

Bleeding: A tourniquet is a way to completely cut off blood flow if bleeding is life threatening. Blood loss is fatal when 40% is gone which is half a gallon or nearly 2 liters. Shock happens well before this. Keep extremities elevated to get blood to the brain. Anything that tightens might help, but a rope or cloth tightened with a stick might give more effect. You must weigh blood loss against saving the limb to determine whether to occasionally let blood flow. Brain cell death occurs five minutes without blood, but other cells are more durable. Some cells can last hours or days, but there may be loss of function. Internal bleeding requires surgery.

Various plants can inhibit bleeding. Astringents constrict blood vessels. See Purple Loosestrife in infections. If applied topically or ingested, it slows all types of bleeding. Topical application is better if the source of bleeding is accessible. See list of anticoagulants under heart palpitations and avoid them until healed.

Suturing / Stitches: A sterilized fishing hook with the barb removed, and fishing line can be used for stitches. Common in the medical world is catgut which stands for cattle gut or cow stomach or intestines that has been purified and braided. The outer most layer of the stomach is used. It is purified with ethyl oxide gas because cooking would destroy it. Using any biological item runs the risk of introducing infection, so weigh the risk. Consider trying on livestock first and see if it produces infection. Tweezers help hold the small needle. The optimal strand length is six times the wound length. For deep cuts, you may need to suture deepest layers first. Many different stitching styles have been used. Tying and cutting each stitch is good for durability, but a continuous stitch is faster. Sutures should be just tight enough to bring the skin together, but not cause whitening of blood loss. Older needles were bone, or a plant thorn. Older threads were flax, hemp, cotton, hair, and other tendons besides catgut. Older threads were unpurified or purified with iodine.

Gangrene: Gangrene is decomposing flesh due to a wound. Gangrene is the same colors as normal bruising but happening in a wound. Oil from walnuts can fight gangrene. Apply walnut oil directly to the infected spot.

Snake bites: Being bitten by a poisonous snake doesn't mean any venom was injected. Snake bites are rarely fatal to healthy adults. Conventional wisdom is to suck out venom, but current wisdom is to let it be. Sucking removes insignificant venom. Anti-venom treatments are dependent upon the type of snake.

Broken bones and sprains: The old saying is that if you can't move it, it is broken. It is true that broken bones can prevent movement due to severe pain in nearby flesh, or loss of the function the bone was providing. However, other diagnostic methods can be used. Key indicators are if the pain is localized along a bone or if there is exceptional local swelling. Pulling on it should cause exceptional pain. Also, sometimes there are muscles spasms. There is no certain way to tell without an X-ray. A sprain can have some of the same symptoms including a cracking sound upon injury, but the pain may be less, and you may have more range of motion. For sprains, treat the pain and swelling for a few days, then begin gentle rehabilitation of the joint and muscles. Some bones can be set, like limb bones, but torso bones like rib bones may have to be babied until they heal. In a cast, the broken bone should not move. When putting on a cast, be sure that circulation is not cut off. Check the limb for good blood flow every couple of hours for one day. Plaster can be made from ground lime, gypsum, clay, or flour, but gypsum is preferred for casts. Gypsum is found in drywall/wallboard and chalk. Gypsum is a crystal found in white to slightly gold or tan sands. It needs to be ground. Also, consider using pine sap as a binder for other inventive cast designs.

Humane euthanasia: If someone is in fatal pain, and if they can eat or drink, painless poison drinks can be given. See fiction stories by the author for ways to do this.

Other emergencies and treatment

Choking: If they are coughing, then let them handle it. If they aren't breathing or become unconscious, perform the Heimlich maneuver. Stand behind. Reach around grabbing your fist in front just below the rib cage. Thrust in and up into the rib cage. Chest thrusts are an alternative. After five unsuccessful thrusts, try five back slaps. Back slaps should be with the palm, between the shoulder blades, and if possible, get the person to lean forward or look down. Return to thrusts after five slaps. With unconscious people, CPR may be necessary. For babies: back thrusts are first with them face down with head at your knees. Support the baby's head with hand on its jaw. Then chest thrusts are second, face up. Use only two fingers to thrust. A slight incline is beneficial in either pose, so mouth is below stomach.

Heart attack: The main sign of a heart attack is pain that spreads to arm, neck and back. Other likely symptoms are shortness of breath, nausea, sweating, and lightheadedness. However, all these symptoms can exist with other causes such as shock. If it is not severe, no action is required immediately, and other causes can be considered. Rule out bleeding syndromes before giving aspirin. (If pain is mostly across the back, don't give aspirin.) If the pulse has stopped or the person becomes unconscious and stops breathing, the CPR can be done.

CPR: For mild heart attack, see above. If they are conscious, you don't need CPR. First, check for circulation signs or signs of life such as breathing, moving, or coughing. If unsure, check for pulse. If they aren't breathing, but have other circulation signs, you can do the breathing recovery with mouth-to-mouth resuscitation. If they have drowned, put on stomach first to remove water.

CPR parts:

1. Rescue breathing: Put person on back, lift head back and check for obstructions, pinch the nose, with mouth over mouth give a full breath, if breath won't go in check for choking. For infants, cover

mouth and nose with mouth. Next, do chest compressions if there are no circulation signs.

2. Chest compressions: place hands on lower rib cage. Keep your arms straight and use leaning to compress the breastbone an inch or two. Do 15 compressions for 2 mouth breaths. After one-minute pause to check for recovery. For young children, use one hand. For babies, use two fingers.

Heart palpitations: Palpitations or irregular heartbeats can be from anxiety, fatigue, or poor heart condition. Relieve those causes. If irregular heartbeats continue for more than a day, blood thinners should be used to lower stroke risk. Aspirin is a mildly effective thinner at any dose. Other natural mild thinners are earthworms, onion, garlic, fish oil, celery, cranberries, soybeans, wheat grass, red clover, turmeric, and bilberry. Also try sour dock root, goldenrod seed, and dried pollen from mace which is a version of a cattail. Avoid excessive eating of greens.

Stethoscope: You can make your own stethoscope to listen to the heartbeat (or lungs). Early stethoscopes were just tubes. Then they became horn-shaped. Finally, long rubber hoses were connected to make the modern version.

Stroke: Symptoms are sudden numbness on one side of the body, trouble speaking and severe headache. Before treatment, rule out ischemic strokes which are bleeding instead of blood clot. Rule out migraines which come on slowly and are milder. Rule out infection which happens more slowly. If ER treatment is not available for a clot, give the maximum dose of aspirin. Ischemic strokes may have the same symptoms, but instead of numbness, there may only be weakness in the body. It may appear like a mild clot stroke. Without advanced equipment, medical history might be your only tool to distinguish a mild clot stroke and initial phases of an ischemic stroke. Ischemic strokes will often worsen with time and there is no easy treatment without advanced equipment. Sickle cell anemia is one risk factor for ischemia, but many other risk factors are the same as for clots. Any of these within a day or so before could indicate ischemia: alcohol overuse, severe infection or flu, or severe psychological states. A previous irregular heartbeat or any other heart problem suggests the stroke is a clot, but it doesn't rule out ischemia. It may be too late for anticoagulants, but see the list under heart palpitations.

Heat exhaustion: Move to cool place, drink water, and eat salty foods. Massage and stretch cramps. To prevent it, work during cool parts of days. Drink water and mist yourself. Don't overeat or drink alcohol. Take a break at the first sign of dizziness, headache, or nausea.

Burns: First and second degree burns affect only the skin. A third-degree burn affects the organs and requires surgery. For a third-degree burn, the skin will be charred. For skin: apply cold cloth for 15 minutes, and then apply aloe. To extract aloe, cut a bottom leaf, split to let yellow sap escape for a few minutes until most is gone or you are out of patience, then squeeze or scrape out the gel to use. In northern US, aloe vera grows best in greenhouses.

Tracheotomy: A tracheotomy is necessary if breathing stops due to blockage. Other serious breathing symptoms are widespread bluish skin, rapid heart rate, headache, confusion, spasms anywhere, but especially in a hand. A tracheotomy has risks, so perform only if there is high risk of death. Intubation may be an alternative, but again it requires skill and has risks. Intubation is to insert a tube through the mouth to the lungs. It keeps open airways. The patient may need to be sedated. To intubate through the mouth to the lungs, the tube would have to pass between the throat, through the larynx to the windpipe. That is difficult without a video scope. Intubation through the nostrils is possible but is less common because smaller tubes are used. A tracheotomy will insert a temporary or permanent pipe into the throat. Cut the skin below the Adam's apple, which is about halfway down the neck. Horizontal incisions are preferred. The trachea or windpipe will be the obvious large tube under the skin. If possible, and if you have time, connect a hook to the trachea to be able to support it open. Locate the cartilage rings around the trachea. Cut horizontally between them if possible. Insert the tube. Close the wound. Many types of scalpels, scissors and other medical devices should be on-hand in case they are needed.

Frostbite or hypothermia: remove wet clothing. May bathe in warm water up to 45 minutes.

Breathing problems
See CPR above. See tracheotomy. See also pneumonia.

Allergies: Wear a mask to reduce inhaling allergens such as pollen and dust. If anaphylaxis, a severe allergy response, occurs, treat with corticosteroids and antihistamines. See below and "infections" for steroids. If you have old antihistamines, the medicine is likely still active but at lower strength, so the required dose is likely higher. I know of no natural antihistamines. Even the first antihistamines required advanced chemistry. There are many theories on allergies. One theory is that the immune system is overactive because it hasn't been exposed to enough real threat. Natural lifestyles increase the exposure of people to a wide variety of natural things such as bacteria. Therefore, after adopting a natural lifestyle, future generations should have very little trouble with allergies. However, in the transition, people with allergies may have problems. One form of treatment is to increase the exposure to allergens very slowly and consistently over months so that the body learns it isn't a threat. For people with severe reactions, attempting this could be hazardous. To gauge tolerance to allergens, use the poison test method.

Asthma: Asthma is usually diagnosed as wheezing, but also listen for long-term coughs and ask about chest tightness. An easy check is measuring for low lung volume by breathing into a bag and comparing to others of the same body size. A stethoscope can be used to listen for wheezing in the lungs (see "other emergencies". Avoidance of infections, allergens, and extreme situations is best. Treatment: remove the cause, sit up, and avoid aspirin. Corticosteroids help. Also, use mulberry root bark, tea from gingko leaves or seeds, and cooked young leaves of stinging nettles. (These don't appear to be steroids.)

Some breathing problems can be improved with other treatments. If mucus is present, physical therapy might help. If lung volume is low, exercising the lung will help. Lying in prone position, on stomach, is probably best, followed by inclined or elevated on back. If fluid is filling lungs, it might be loosened by humidity or vapor coming off of a steaming pot. Physical therapy is done with clapping hand motions. Clapping should not be painful or sting. Also try vibrating the hand placed over the lung. There are several positions for each part of the lung. While sitting, clap vertically on the shoulders. While sitting and leaning forward, clap the shoulder blades. While lying on the back, clap below the collar bone. Lay on the side and clap the lower ribs. Turn at various angles from prone to on back so each direction can be treated. After a few

minutes of therapy in a single position, have the patient breathe
deeply and attempt to cough. Then move to the next position.
Don't do while food is being digested. Modern medicines have
very little improvement on coughing. It can be hard to get the right
dose for herbal medicines for coughing, and having the wrong dose
can be a big risk when they affect breathing. A tea from raspberry
leaves and roots can be a decongestant. Onions and garlic can be an
expectorant. Onions and garlic used as medicine may have to be
eaten raw. Chives might be found more reliably. Although medical
use of chives isn't documented, it is a close relative to onions.

Hiccups: Pull on tongue. Drink water quickly. For children, drink
milk instead.

Gastro-intestinal problems

Generally, eat fibrous foods and drink lots of water. Additionally,
deal with mental causes since the GI tract is very responsive to
emotion.

Diarrhea: The normal guidance to deal with diarrhea is to go on
BRAT diet, which is bananas, rice, apples, toast. These may not be
available. Oats are also known to slow down the system.
Astringents, such as purple loosestrife, constrict all flow. (See
section on infections).

Painful gas: Walk it off. Try to make no sudden changes in diet.

Heartburn and reflux: Heart burn is called that because it can feel
like a heart attack without other relevant symptoms. Eat smaller,
more frequent meals. Avoid pain killers. Avoid alcohol. Incline
bed so the head is higher. There are various theories about whether
someone with heartburn should increase or decrease stomach acid to
relieve heartburn. Try antacids, including apple cider vinegar, and
bark of beech trees. Alternatively, try hot peppers, ginger, and
acidic foods. For ulcers, use plantain leaves. Try mint leaves.

Constipation: It is less likely to be a concern when eating natural
foods. Laxatives comes in variation between mild and purging.
Water and walking help. Examples of mild laxatives are celery,
burdock, mustard, and parsley.

Hemorrhoids can be treated by eating a small amount of hot
peppers. Also considering boiling the whole thistle plant to make a
topical medicine.

Parasites in the gut such as hookworm can be expelled by eating onions. Try raw. Symptoms of gut parasites are the same as any lower GI issues. If symptoms persist, try the remedy. Also try carrots, locust tree stem and root bark, walnut tree leaves, or whole ground pumpkin seeds with husk.

Ear, Nose and Throat

Earaches could be caused by many things, so the cause needs to be identified. If ear drainage is a problem that can be relieved by yawning or chewing. Gently blowing the nose might help, but a strong blow will likely make it worse. Use a light and magnifying glass to inspect ears. A hooked tool is effective at removing wax.

Sinus drainage causes sore throats and laryngitis and can be a cause of earaches. Be sure to get enough water. Another cause of sore throats and laryngitis is acid reflux. See pain management for throat pain. To prevent symptoms, use a nasal irrigator. Use salt in the water, or a mixture with baking soda if you have it. If the salt causes stinging, try a lower dose. A clay pot with a spout could be made to irrigate. However, putting the water in cupped hand and breathing in the liquid should work too.

Ringing ears normally aren't a health concern unless it occurs with other symptoms. Hearing loss is most often due hearing loud noises. Except for gunfire, life will be quiet. Use hearing protection when using guns. For the hard of hearing, an ear trumpet could be made. An ear trumpet is any horn-shaped funnel and could be made from an animal horn or carved wood.

Nosebleeds are normally not a health concern. Pinch the bridge of the nose.

Eyes

Before eyeglasses, rounded gems were used to magnify reading material. Myopia or near-sightedness is more common in people who don't play outside, but who stay inside and read or play video games. There are other causes of eye problems. However, if people worked more outside, the demand for eyeglasses is reduced. Eye exercises are controversial because there isn't clear evidence that they work to correct vision. If you can find eyeglasses, you won't find one that exactly matches your need. Overdoing it can damage vision, so pick one that under corrects. Binoculars can be adjusted to any magnification, so they can always be used by people with myopia to see distant objects.

Cataracts occur in people in 60s or older. Vision is cloudy, and pupils may look white. Corrective lenses may help. Exposure to UV light and lack of proper nutrition can be causes.

Macular degeneration appears as chronic cloudy or dark spots on the center of the eye. Among the causes are exposure to UV light and lack of proper nutrition.

UV: In the US, sunglasses are required to have UV filters, so use them if you have them. Look for U400. Eyeglasses may have filters, especially if they are polycarbonate versus glass or plastic. Smoky quartz has been used as material for sunglasses. It is a brownish gray crystal. A brimmed hat is effective at reducing UV light coming to the eyes. When not facing the sun, most UV light coming to the eyes still comes from the sky, but from the same process that makes the sky blue. The brim stops UV because it covers part or all the sky. Use the hat or avoid times with a high UV index which is mid-summer, mid-day, with no cloud cover. Ground surfaces can reflect UV light such as water surfaces and snow. Also, pavement and other manufactured surfaces tend to have higher UV reflection than plants. So, avoid those conditions. Avoid any sunny day with snow on the ground. Painful eyes after being outside could be snow blindness or its equivalent in summer, so sit in a dark room and keep eyes moist. Snow goggles can be used when it is necessary to work on bright days outside on the snow in winter or near water in summer. Snow goggles are shaped like glasses but are solid except for horizontal slits which limit the light coming to the eye. Snow goggles can be made from anything such as wood, bone, antler, or reed grass. Snow goggles can be temporally removed if you need to bait a hook while fishing.

Pink eye is a viral infection in the eye which causes it to be more bloodshot than other irritation. Also, pus may come out. It should go away in three weeks if viral. Be careful not to infect others. Antibiotic eye drops help if it is bacteriological. Bacterial, parasitic and fungal infections are usually localized verses viral are throughout the body.

Sties in the eyelid are painful bumps. It is a clogged oil gland. It normally goes away in a couple days. Warm compress might help with discomfort.

Epilepsy and Seizures

Epilepsy can be genetic or caused by stroke, infection, overuse of antibiotics, sleep deprivation, deficiency of vitamin B, medical or visual overstimulation, or trauma to the head. The main symptom is a seizure. The main immediate treatment is to keep the patient from injuring themselves. An experience epileptic may learn the signs that a seizure is going to occur so can take steps for safety. If the cause is infection of vitamin B deficiency, then treat that. Most epilepsy cases will go away if the cause is removed. Consuming large amounts of alcohol can cause or relieve epilepsy, but the increase may be due to interference with standard medicines for epilepsy. Eating a diet that is nearly exclusively fats is known to relieve epilepsy, but it will have long-term health consequences. Be cautious to watch for signs of depression in long-term cases.

Infection

Before modern science and lifestyles, infections were the greatest health problem. Vaccines and medical science made infection less of a concern, but then lifestyle diseases took over.

Soap: To make lye soap, use hardwood ashes. Leach lye by soaking the ashes in water for a couple days. A lye and water solution results. Lye is dangerous so use goggles and gloves. Make a system so there is no risk of splashing. Then add the lye to any oil, but food oil is better. Evaporate the soapy liquid until it is the consistency you want for laundry detergent versus hand soap. Alternatively, some plants make a soap-like substance. An example is the horse chestnut or buckeye. The buckeye might be useable as a bar of soap but leaching out the soap gives a liquid form. Also, try yucca root.

Fever from infectious disease is usually self-limiting. Fever is a natural reaction to infection to change the body temperature to make it more effective at fighting the infection. No treatment for fever is necessary, but pain and discomfort can be treated with mild pain killers. Fever from another cause exceeding 104 in others should be treated. (Some doctors recommend other limits for treatment.) Watch for seizures. Water, even if not refrigerated, is cooling either through submersion (because water temperature is lower than a fever) or if water is sprayed on because it will evaporate.

Healing wounds: Skin infections with pus heal more quickly if pus is extracted. Other people should be careful not to be exposed to the pus since it can be infectious. Also, remove dead tissue. An exception is that blisters heal better when not opened. Fly maggots are sometimes used for removal of difficult to get out dead tissue. Some fly maggots might introduce more pathogens than they remove. The only known species of fly used for this is Calliphorid (blow flies), but those flies can still carry disease from carrion they feed on. House flies are not Calliphoridae. Calliphoridae have a shiny metallic appearance that are blue or green.

Tetanus bacteria are common in soil and manure. The bacteria normally require a break in the skin to enter. Therefore, see the issue of footwear. Severe muscle spasms lasting minutes is the strongest symptom. Often spasms start with lock jaw, but the whole body can convulse at once. It can be severe enough to break bones or be fatal. Muscle stretching is the practical way to relieve tension when antibiotics are not available. You may have to help them do yoga while they are reclined. Try muscle relaxers. If trading relationships with groups with vaccine technology exist, a tetanus vaccine is a high priority. Incubation: 3 days to 3 weeks.

Footwear is relevant to health. If you are walking inside or on clean paths, walking barefoot is normally helpful for feet. However, cuts on the feet often result in tetanus. Footwear protects you against other parasites in the soil too. Hookworm is more common in warmer, wetter climates, and will absorb through skin of bare feet.

Communicable disease: Nearly all infectious diseases in humans come from animals. Examples are swine flu and avian flu. The disease is most likely transferred to humans through living close to animals, such as in the same building, unsanitary practices, or handling dead animals incorrectly and eating the meat that isn't cooked. Some diseases will cause visible signs on a dead animal such as spots on the liver. See food handling methods to be safe. Communicable disease is transferred human to human via cough or sneeze droplets, breath droplets, touch including sexual, and through waste.

Most communicable disease is bacterial or viral, but pneumonia also can be fungal or parasitic. Viral infections are normally throughout the whole body because viruses easily travel through the bloodstream. However, bacterial infections are mostly localized because bacteria don't easily go through the body. An ear infection or strep throat are examples of bacterial infections. Bacterial infections can be treated with antibiotics if the symptoms are bad. Otherwise, immunity develops over time.

Strategies to avoid infectious diseases are isolation, inoculation with vaccines, and using other protection. Protections depend on the way the infection is transmitted. Droplets are stopped by masks and distance. Human and animal waste is curbed through sanitation. Influenza or flu is an example of how a disease is prevented by immunity. Newest versions of the flu are normally less severe because of immunity from similar viruses. If vaccination is not available, consider variolation, deliberate infection to bring immunity (see next paragraph). See warnings of using aspirin in children with flu.

Smallpox has been eradicated. However, contact with the carrier animal species could reintroduce it to humans. Smallpox are bumps over the whole body. First symptoms are fever and vomiting. Second is rash and mouth sores. Third is rash becoming fluid-filled blisters over the whole body. The person may look like a reptile with scales. Death rate is 30%, and higher among babies. Exposure is through large droplets that travel only a few feet. Exposure risk is usually worse during the first phases. Vaccination is relatively easy by variolation but still have a 1% mortality rate. Variolation is to give a mild infection with the live virus. Variolate by exposing a scab or pus from an infected person to a small scratch on the skin of a healthy person. The infection will likely remain local but produce an immune response. The size and depth of scratch, amount of pus, and exposure to the mouth and nose could be factors in controlling strength of immune response and the risk of getting the full infection. Consider bandaging the scratch to prevent aerial dispersion. It takes time for symptoms to develop and treatment before then can be helpful. For example, variolation may still reduce symptoms later even for people who've already been infected in the last three days. Incubation: 1-3 weeks, infectious: Until no symptoms.

Tuberculosis, or consumption, is a bacterial disease in the lungs. Symptoms are coughing mucus with blood, fever, night sweats, and other symptoms depending on if it spreads. TB is spread with small droplets including spitting up mucus, so masks and large distances are required. Swallow mucus. Treatment is with antibiotics for months. Additionally, many types of clovers have a beneficial effect on lymph issues in TB. Since leaves and flowers of clover are edible unless moldy, there is little risk to trying this treatment. Similar effects have been found from waterlily rhizome, mustard leaves and flowers, clematis leaves and flowers, and wintergreen leaves. Also try fir, spruce and pine tree pitch or bark made into a tea. Incubation: roughly a month, infectious: weeks after symptoms and may reappear much later. TB may cause meningitis. Aspirin isn't recommended for meningitis, but is sometimes helpful if TB causes it.

Measles is a flat rash that spreads from the face to the rest of the body. Initial symptoms may include white spots in mouth, fever, cough, runny nose, and irritated eyes. Diarrhea, earache, and pneumonia may occur. There is a small chance of many other severe complications, especially in the brain. Treat the symptoms. Death is more common in the malnourished. People are most infectious before the rash and into the first days of the rash. Transmission is through droplets. Variolation was performed by taking eye drops from an infected person and putting on a scratch. A week or so later, mild symptoms should appear. The disease not being severe for most people. However, since a few people will have problems, it is worth preventative medicine. Incubation: 10-12 days, infectious: 4 days after symptoms start.

Rubella: Rubella is also called German Measles but is not the same. It is a virus spread by coughs, so wear a mask unless your goal is herd immunity. In that case expose all young children to the patient. Skin rash is milder than measles since it lasts three days. Bleeding may occur, as well as swelling, and nerves in the skin may misfire giving wrong signals such as numbness. Pregnancy complications can occur if the woman is early in term. Incubation: 2 weeks, infectious: 1 week after symptoms start, but babies born with it are infectious for a year. Pregnant women should wear masks if they are not immune.

Whooping cough or pertussis is a severe cough lasting months. Severe coughs may damage the body in many ways over time, also there is a risk of difficulty breathing and pneumonia. Symptoms are similar to a cold, but with the cough sounding like a "whoop". It is caused by a bacterium spread in large droplets. Treatment is with antibiotics. See the section on breathing problems. Vaccination for bacteriological infection is with whole, dead cells of the bacteria, but isolating bacteria, killing it, and performing an inoculation are all difficult. Isolating them, killing them, and performing an inoculation are all difficult. Incubation: commonly 1 to 2 weeks but can be longer. Infectious: Usually 3 weeks.

Meningitis is severe headache followed by severe neck stiffness preventing forward movement of the head. Fever and mental changes are common. Leg flexibility, rash, skin color and circulation may also be affected. Meningitis can be bacteriological, viral, or fungal. It spread through droplets, but usually not so easily spread and sometimes requires fecal contamination. Antibiotics might prevent transfer if you have been exposed. Mortality rate is high. Treatment is with antibiotics and steroids if the cause could be bacteriological, and with antifungal if the cause could be fungal. There are no easy ways to tell which type it is, but bacterial or viral will have a transmission history from others. Viral is most common. Severity is lower if viral. Incubation: bacterial is usually 2-10 days, infectious: assume is same as symptoms.

Hepatitis B is a virus that affects the liver. If it shows symptoms, it will be vomiting, yellow skin, tiredness, dark urine, and abdominal pain that appears 1 to 6 months after exposure. Cirrhosis may also occur with or without other symptoms. Infection is through body fluids. Sexual intercourse and mosquitos are two ways of fluid transfer. The only treatment is time. Incubation: up to 6 months. Infectious: assume same as symptoms.

Cirrhosis can be from alcoholism, Hepatitis B, lifestyle diseases, and overuse of steroids. Initial symptoms can include tiredness, loss of appetite, and abdominal pain on upper right. Symptoms developing over time include loss in mental abilities, swelling legs, dark urine, yellow or itchy skin, red palms, spider veins, and lastly a swelling abdomen or breast of men. Many patients recover without medical treatment other than removing the cause. Alcoholic cirrhosis is treated by abstinence from alcohol. If a secondary bacteriological infection occurs, antibiotic may help.

Plague from Yersinia Pestis. Black Death begins as fever, weakness, and headache a few days after exposure. It has three forms: bubonic, septicemic, and pneumonic. In pneumonic, additional symptoms are shortness of breath, cough, and chest pain. In bubonic form, lymph nodes swell. In septicemic form, tissues turn black and die from inability to control internal bleeding. Yersinia Pestis is a bacterium spread from animals by flea bites. Once in human it is spread by droplet. Droplet transfer causes the pneumonic form and is 100% fatal. Other forms of transfer are common, such as contact with body fluids. The pneumonic form can occur from a patient infecting themselves. Antibiotics often help with septicemic form. Prevention is by control of rodents and flies, and wearing masks prevents droplet spread. Also, there is a wife's tale that eating garlic pickled in red wine vinegar wards off the bacteria. Incubation: 1-3 days, infectious: assumed to be 3 weeks.

Typhus is a bacterial infection. Symptoms are fever, headache, and rash about a week after exposure. The rash starts on torso and works outward. Symptoms similar to meningitis may begin later. Various versions of the bacteria are spread either by body lice, chigger, or fleas. See above for lice and chiggers. Control fleas and chiggers by controlling rodents and other animals. Typhus is often fatal. Treatment is with antibiotics. Incubation: 1-2 weeks.

Anthrax: Anthrax is a bacteriological infection. It can happen on the skin or in lungs and GI tract. On the skin, it starts as a blister that grows into a painless black lesion. Infection is most likely from animals, but infected people should be put in quarantine because even if chance of transmission is low, the consequences are high. On the skin, infection occurs through a scrape. The GI form is bloody diarrhea. Death is possible in skin and GI forms if untreated. Respiratory anthrax is similar to the flu but continues to worsen. Flu without contact with another person with flu, but by someone that handles animals should be viewed as having anthrax. Respiratory anthrax is nearly always fatal. Treatment is done rapidly with antibiotics. To prevent, see livestock. Also, all people dealing with animals should have all scrapes properly bandaged and treated. Incubation: 1 day to 2 months. Infectious: Assume it is same as symptoms.

Cholera: Cholera is a bacteriological infection of the small intestine producing diarrhea. Some patients may have mild cases, but death is possible. Children are more susceptible. It is spread by unsanitary conditions such as contact with feces. Treatment is through rehydration and antibiotics. Treatments that soothe the colon may help. Try a salty rice broth of rice not grown in sandy soil so it has high zinc. Incubation: hours to 5 days, Infectious: Average is 5 days after symptoms start.

Polio: Poliomyelitis is a bacterial infection spread by fecal matter and occasionally by saliva. Polio causes severe reactions in about one-percent of people infected. The most severe reaction is partial paralysis. Milder symptoms are flu-like. Symptoms seem to be worse in people with weakened immune systems. Polio vaccine is a weakened version of the virus. Treat like the flu to prevent pneumonia. Incubation: 1 week to 1 month, Infectiousness: several weeks.

Rotavirus is a virus that is transmitted through feces. Nearly every child gets this by age five, so is immune, but vaccines can prevent it. Rotavirus is a stomach flu. Treat the symptoms. Incubation: 2 days, Infectiousness: 19 days.

Diphtheria is a bacteriological infection. It begins as a sore throat or fever. Lymph nodes in the neck may swell. In severe cases, paralysis can result. Treat with antibiotics. Antibiotics may also reduce transmission. Bacteria are transmitted through large droplets, so wear masks. Many other symptoms can happen such as white splotches in mouth, throat and nose or lesions on the legs. Breathing may become difficult because of swelling or lesions. See "emergency" for tracheotomy. Incubation: 2-5 days, infectiousness: thought to be 4 weeks.

Mumps is a virus. First symptoms are most commonly fever and headache. Then the saliva gland swells out of the bottom of the chin. Many organs, especially the testes and breasts may become inflamed. No treatment is recommended. If possible, avoid using aspirin. Incubation: 7-25 days, infectious: 8 days after symptoms start.

Varicella: Chicken pox is small itchy blisters that start on head and torso. Because adult men have it more severely, such as getting pneumonia, children were often intentionally infected by exposure. If possible, avoid using aspirin. Treat with anti-itch. Incubation: 10-21 days, infectious: usually 5 days after symptoms start.

Leprosy or Hansen's disease: Leprosy is caused by bacteria and so is spread through close human contact. Symptoms: Pink patches on skin is often the first symptom. Nerve damage may occur in the patches or in fingers and toes. Over long term, look for thickening of skin, change of voice, and joint or cartilage problems. Normally symptoms appear after five years. Yet, the range is between one and twenty years for symptoms to appear. Treatment: Some antibiotics may have an effect on leprosy. Regardless, keeping the patient in good health will reduce transmission and antibiotics are likely to help with relevant healing. Antibiotics can control secondary infections. To help lesions to heal, treat them like wounds. Topical antivirals or antiseptics may help lesions. Prevention: Family members of people with leprosy are advised to take precautions. The two most common means of transfer of the bacteria are through nasal discharge and skin shedding. For nasal discharge, cover sneezes, disinfect clothing or bedding infected by sneezes, wash hands, and dispose or disinfect handkerchiefs. For skin shedding, frequently wipe dust from areas where the person sits, and frequently beat rugs or bedding outside. There are two possible paths of infection. Infection through skin may require that the person have a skin abrasion for the bacteria to enter the body. Therefore, treat and bandage all small wounds on family members. However, infection into the nose may be possible, so washing hands by unaffected people is imperative. Since the disease has a very long incubation time, you couldn't know if someone else in the family got it from the patient. Inspecting newcomers for lesions may not be effective because of the long incubation time. In areas where leprosy is common, many people have immunity to it. This shows that it is commonly transferred, but it doesn't always cause the disease. People susceptible to autoimmune and Parkinson's disease are also more susceptible develop leprosy, but others are less likely to get it. It appears that inflammation allows leprosy to overcome defenses. Survivors of tuberculosis are often moderately protected against leprosy. Both tuberculosis and leprosy are mycobacterium so the body might be trained to fight both. That suggests infecting with tuberculosis would vaccinate against leprosy, but one problem with that is TB would likely increase the inflammation level and let leprosy invade. Therefore, treat inflammation in all people who have contact with the patient, and everyone else too. For the general population: treat all wounds. Serve anti-inflammatory foods and apply relevant medicines. It is a difficult ethical issue about quarantining a whole family for their lifetimes, but people with an inflammatory condition might want to isolate themselves.

Whipworm: Not properly handling human waste or not making compost safe can transfer parasitic disease such as Trichuriasis which causes bloody diarrhea. Washing vegetables reduces exposure. A minor infection may be no concern. See other deworming methods for treatment.

Trematoda: Flatworms have the same cause and prevention as whipworms. Additionally, it comes from unclean drinking water.

Night blindness is a distinguishing symptom. This is more likely in tropical areas.

Leptospirosis or Black Jaundice is a disease from exposure to bacteria mostly found in rat urine. Symptoms appear one to two weeks after exposure. Red eyes are the most common symptom. The first phase lasts a day to a week, and symptoms include fever, chills, headache, muscle aches, and abdominal pain. The headache is a throbbing pain in the front or temples. Sensitivity to light is related. Aches are mostly likely in calf muscles or lower back. There may be a cough, or GI symptoms. Between the phases there may be a short recovery, but this is the eye of the hurricane. The second phase kicks in and lasts a week to a month. Meningitis occurs in the second phase. This can cause a wide range of related problems such as nose bleeds, coughing blood, black stools, and weakness or paralysis in one side of the body. If lungs fill with blood, death is likely. Prevention: Sanitation and rat extermination. Avoid contact with farm animals if they have been infected. Treatment: Use an antibiotic. The earlier it is given, the better. Treat symptoms such as dehydration if GI is involved. If the patient's feces are handled properly, there is little risk to others. If exposure is suspected, antibiotic can be given to ward it off. Some people have tried corticosteroids, but with uncertain benefit. Recovered patients may have long lasting fatigue or eye problems.

Neurocysticercosis: This is a tapeworm from pigs. Symptoms do not occur until the disease is severe. Symptoms include seizures, headaches, blindness, meningitis, and dementia. Treat the symptoms. Prevent by keeping wild boar away. Properly cook pork. Caring for pigs requires special care.

Mosquito and tick diseases: There are many more insect-borne diseases in the tropics. Diseases are commonly bacteriological but can be other types. Bacterial diseases will spread from a growing rash near the bug bite. They can be treated with antibiotics. Encephalitis is common beyond the tropics. It is a virus that causes fever, headaches. There can be many other symptoms such as stiff neck that is consistent with encephalitis depending on which version of the virus is gotten. Treat the symptoms. If joint pain occurs, avoid using joints to prevent damage. Can be fatal. Control mosquitos and birds around your home. Another mosquito disease is spotted fever. Spotted fevers start the same as other bacteriological infections but produce many small bleedings spots all over the body. Muscle spasms should be treated with physical therapy because severe spasm can deform body parts. Hot compresses help therapy. Antispasmodics reduce damage.

Eastern equine encephalitis (EEE) is common in birds, and mosquitos transfer it to horses and humans. The most common symptom of EEE is sleepiness. Treat with steroids, antispasmodics, aspirin, and fluids. Be watchful for breathing difficulties. Brain damage is likely. Especially harmful to children.

Malaria was common in the United States in all areas except the dry parts of the west and mountainous areas. In was eradicated by the 1950s except for local outbreaks by widespread spraying, installing window screens and improving drainage conditions. Still, thousands of people in the US contract malaria per year. Therefore, malaria can spread again, first through the South, but then elsewhere, if controls are no longer used. Symptoms begin a week to a month after a bite. It is a parasitic disease. Initial symptoms include flu-like symptoms, plus joint pain, jaundice, and convulsions. Cycles of fever and chills happen over periods of days compared to with the flu over a few hours. More severe symptoms might develop such as neurological problems, especially with eyes and muscles. There may be trouble breathing or the urine may be black. Treat the symptoms. Babesiosis is similar to malaria but spread by ticks, and it is treated the same. Quinine is the bark of the cinchona tree. Tonic water in bars is made from cinchona and contains quinine. Cinchona is a tropical plant with hairy bark and is evergreen leaves. Similar plants grow elsewhere in the same family and have similar effects. Look for shrubs with multi-branched flower clusters that are white to red. Also, aspirin helps. Try cannabis, lilac bark, ash tree bark, tea from stinging nettle leaves, and dried root bark from dogwoods. People who are repeatedly bitten by infected mosquitos can develop some immunity, but it takes being bitten by infected mosquitos every year or so to keep it active. However, even with immunity, anemia is a long-term risk.

Dengue Fever: Dengue is in a general class of viruses that cause hemorrhagic fever. The larger group includes Ebola and Marburg. Aedes Aegypti mosquitoes normally live below 35 degrees North. That includes the deep south in the US, but their range can expand to the mid-South if temperatures rise. They are the primary carrier of dengue fever. Symptoms begin a few days to two weeks after a bite. Symptoms include fever, headache, and vomiting. A mild rash occurs over the whole body. Rash may be flat or slightly raised. One confirming test: use a blood pressure cuff inflated halfway between the patient's two BP numbers for five minutes. It is positive if it leaves ten or more red spots per square inch on the tested limb. A quick version of the test is to press hard with one finger. Also, be wary of increased fluid flow such as saliva or bleeding from nose or any other opening. Internal bleeding may cause death from loss of blood or filling of lungs. Watch for dropping BP. Many viral hemorrhagic fevers are usually highly infectious as well as dangerous. Extreme precautions, of all sorts, need to be taken. Dispose or sanitize of anything that comes into contact with the patient. Wear gloves and rigorously sanitize them. Isolate the patient into their own building or if pleasant outside put them under a tent. Health care workers should use the absolute best mask or air filtration system they have. Isolate anyone that has had contact with the patient and develops headache or fever. Treatment of mild cases is with intake of fluids like with diarrhea. Try an antiviral if you have one. See below. Aspirin may increase bleeding, so avoid. The risk is over in a few days. Treatment with blood pressure medicine is helpful to prevent bleeding. It may be counter-intuitive since dropping blood pressure is a warning sign of serious complication, but that happens because of constricted blood vessels. See BP meds below. Cannabis helps with respiratory distress which is sometimes a complication. Flavivirus infections such as Zika, Yellow Fever, and West Nile Virus are similar to Dengue. Red eyes are more likely with Zika. Rash is usually raised. Zika is usually mild except for on unborn children. West Nile Virus is more likely to have excessive sweating, and GI symptoms, but rashes are less common. Aspirin is fine for WNV. Yellow Fever is more likely to have fever that comes and goes, loss of appetite, and muscle pain, especially in the back. Yellow skin, and bleeding from orifices comes later and is a serious sign. The mosquito that transmits these diseases, Aedes Aegypti is common in the day and night. Rehydrate the patient. Carefully weigh the need for pain relief against the possibility of bleeding, but that is a problem in the second phase.

Scarlet fever is caused by the strep bacteria. One form of it is strep throat, but it should be taken seriously. Symptoms are a bumpy red tongue, rash anywhere but especially cheeks that feels like sandpaper, red lines in joint creases, typical cold and flu symptoms with a sore throat. The tongue often looks white before the rash develops on it, and the white coat will eventually shed off. The tongue is often the first symptom with rash developing later. Treat with antibiotics to prevent complications which can be fatal in children. Infants and toddlers may only have mild symptoms. Treat the sore throat. To prevent transfer of the infection, treat like a cold. Incubation time is one day to one week. Most severe symptoms and infectiousness last a week or two. Quarantining for two weeks is preferable to alternatives. Vaccines were never developed but in early outbreaks, immunization with killed bacteria was done. Killed bacteria were produced by isolating one in a lab specimen, growing in the lab in a solution of mammal pancreas, and then heating to and holding at 37 degrees Celsius for three days. Killed bacteria were put into skin or into nose.

Pneumonia has many causes. Pneumonia is usually diagnosed by breathing difficulty. Compare to other breathing problems to clarify diagnosis. Also check for productive cough, fever. Wheezing is possible with pneumonia, but less likely than other breathing problems. Viral pneumonia is the exception where wheezing is more likely. Vitamin deficiency may increase risk of getting pneumonia. Treatment: Antibiotics can help if it is bacterial. Laying in prone position, on stomach, is probably best, followed by inclined or elevated on back. People with pneumonia may be too exhausted to exercise their lungs or it may cause stabbing pain but try breathing exercises to see if they improve. If diseases causing pneumonia are present, preventative vitamin C and lung conditioning may improve outcomes. See the section on breathing problems.

Rabies is a virus. Bats are the carrier for rabies. Bat houses should be in quiet areas away from residences, so contact with bats is uncommon. However, if a bat is on the ground, it should be buried. Dogs can get rabies from bats on the ground, and then infect humans. Put a fence around the bottom of bat houses to keep dogs away. Keep dogs leashed or in pens unless they are working. Observe for changes in behavior. Watch for tiredness, agitation, loss of coordination, and increased saliva production. Tiredness could be old age or summer heat. Drooling could be poor dental care. However, if unexplained symptoms appear, put down your dog, or confine to a sturdy cage. If bitten or scratched by an infected animal, washing for 15 minutes in soap and water may prevent infection. Otherwise, rabies is nearly always fatal. It can take days to years for symptoms to appear depending on the amount of virus transferred. Most commonly, symptoms appear in a couple months. Initial symptoms in humans are like West Nile Virus and encephalitis. If symptoms appear, it is too late. Death occurs roughly a week after symptoms appear because the patient goes into a coma.

Prevention, control, and medicines:

When quarantine or mask wearing is recommended, the times vary. The quarantine lasts for the infectious period of the disease. Wearing masks by the community should continue until it is certain that no one else has been infected. Many diseases have no symptoms in some people. Therefore, it can be a very long time before there is confidence that the disease has been eliminated. One possibility is to continue precautions through two incubation time periods so that the likelihood of people with silent symptoms has been reduced. Some diseases are more severe, so you may want to wait longer. If no other guide is available on infectiousness, assume it is the same as the time span of symptoms. In bacteriological diseases that are effectively treated by antibiotics, time span of symptoms and infectiousness both reduce.

Control:

Infectious diseases are most likely to come from domesticated animals or rodents. The infection can be transferred directly or through a vector such as ticks, fleas and mosquitos.

The most effective way to control mice and rats is to store food in containers. Plastic 1 mm thick or less can be eaten through easily, but over 2 mm, hard plastic is usually safe. Squirrels can eat through even thin metal if they are strongly motivated to do so. Mice and rats are often hidden during the day, but squirrels can be hunted. Cats are natural killers of mice. Dogs chase rats. Doberman Pinchers and Terriers are specialized at killing rats. Other means of catching are traps and cages with bait and glue traps. Dispose of the carcass promptly by burial so that fleas are killed too. Regularly inspect for burrows.

Owls can also control mice. Keep owl houses away from your main areas of activity. Put an owl house on a tree. Make it like a plain, large bird house with a big hole and front porch of roosting branches.

Pets should be indoor only or outdoor only. They are susceptible to many of the same diseases and can bring them inside.

Bug repellent: Work outside during the mid-day during warm dry times. Wear long netting for clothes and any long clothes. Light colored clothes attract mosquitos less. DEET is a powerful insect repellent, but it is difficult to manufacture. Most mosquitos are worse at night.

Citronella oil is a natural mosquito repellant. The oil is made from the lemongrass plant. Even though it is natural, it is better to apply all chemicals to clothing rather than skin to avoid unnecessary exposure. Identification: it is a tall grass with lemon scent. It is not native to North America but might be ornamental. Mosquitos stay away from the grass. It is uncertain if anyone has tried burning the grass. Also try on the skin: lavender oil, tea tree oil, and black pepper oil. Nettles soaked in water for a couple weeks produce a liquid that might deter mosquitos. Consuming mint or garlic might help.

Flies are attracted to meat and feces. Flies and fleas carry disease from one animal to the next. In addition to diseases above, they also carry dysentery (diarrhea) and eye inflammation. When butchering meat, dispose of all extra parts immediately. Bury feces or put a tight-fitting seat on outhouses. Other food waste should be dealt with. Keep farm animals away from your living areas and take away feces. Bathe pets frequently in warm soapy water. Carpets would require vacuuming, but hard floors can be swept. A form of ground white rock, diatomaceous earth, has been used as flea powder, but use a mask so you don't inhale it. For flies, use window screens, flyswatters, and try making fly paper from glue. Control rodents. A Venus flytrap may be hard to keep alive, but it will eat a few flies. A flytrap can be made with a plastic bottle. The best design is to cut off the top and turn over to point it down. In the cap, poke a whole large enough for flies to get into. Put bait in the vessel. Some flies are attracted to blood, sugar, or apple cider vinegar. Flies won't be able to find a way to escape. You could also make this with two pieces of pottery.

A mosquito trap can be made similar to a fly trap. These things may be worth trying, but no guarantees. Option 1: use same overturned bottle but use bait of sugar and yeast. Option 2: Open still water with lots of liquid soap. Mosquitos breed in stagnant still water, and the soap makes them drown.

Control disease from animals by keeping standing water away from homes. Keep animals away from homes, especially squirrels, rats, mice, and birds. Properly handle and cook all meat. Mosquitos usually stay within a couple hundred feet of their nest. Mosquitos only need a tablespoon of still water. Tall vegetation may be enough to trap water for mosquito breeding.   Check if downspouts are draining. Keeping livestock increases your exposure to disease. Remove ticks immediately and you will likely avoid disease. Two species that you should encourage around your home are bats and swallows because they eat mosquitos, so build a home for each. A bat box should be wood, long, and thin with a large opening at the bottom. Place in the sun on a pole. Painting dark may keep it warm. Replace when wood gets old. Barn swallows love rafters of barns to build nests in because they have a roof over their head, and rafters to hold the nest, but they will enjoy typical birdhouses or bird hotels.

Mosquitos can develop at 60 degrees or higher, but prefer weather in the 70s.

Strategies to keep vegetation low: Mow with gas mower, mow with electric mower powered by solar panels, use a mechanical push reel mower, burn the grass if you are sure you can control the fire, have livestock eat the grass and then rake up droppings, and use a scythe.

Medicines:

Steroids: Corticosteroids regulate inflammation. They have a beneficial effect in many disorders where the body needs to be mobilized to respond. They are produced in adrenal cortex of animals. Adrenal cortex is the outer part of the adrenal gland which is the top of the kidney. Potassium naturally increases cortisol levels. Sources of potassium are soybeans and other beans, nuts especially almonds and pistachios, milk, potatoes, beet greens, yams, apricots, parsley, dandelion greens, bran, and bananas. Potassium overdose can be an issue, but the symptoms are not normally severe except for irregular heartbeat. Additionally, licorice increases cortisol. Licorice is the dried roots of the licorice bean plant. Cortisol is a stress hormone, so causing stress will increase it. Intense exercise may give a short-term boost of cortisol, but mild to moderate exercise will lower it. In the long-term, a modern diet, such as refined sugar, increases cortisol. Vitamin C naturally reduces cortisol, but other parts of the same fruits could have positive effects, so the recommendation is undecided on this.

Being a stress hormone, it is harmful if too much is taken. Therefore, only use when needed. Pharmaceutical production of steroids is complicated.

Anti-spasmodic: Try okra seeds, maple bark, onion and garlic bulbs, chamomile, columbine, oats, cannabis, nut grass tubers, poppy, buckwheat, fennel, mint(s), and peony root. Unfortunately, how to use it isn't always certain.

Anti-fungal: Try consuming raw leaves from black medick or alfalfa. The bitter taste is directly related to the anti-fungal benefit. Black medick is a clover that often grows near Dutch white clover but has yellow flowers in small tight bunches and black seeds. Alfalfa is taller with purple flower bunches. Caution: this will also reduce protein digestion and cause blood problems. Watch for side effects: excessive hunger, swollen joints, butterfly rash on cheek bones, mouth ulcers and fatigue. Avoid during pregnancy. Cooking leaves and changing the water so bitterness is gone makes them edible, but also removes the anti-fungal benefit. Leaves can be dried and cooked later for food. Seeds can be sprouted in water twelve hours. Soapy sap from plants like goldenrod are good for external, mouth and vaginal fungus, but avoid swallowing much of it.

Rubbing alcohol: I believe these can be put on the skin, but test in small quantities. Otherwise, they'd just be used for burning or cleaning. You can make alcohol from Queen Anne's lace root and potatoes. Wood alcohol is difficult to make.

Anti-inflammatory: One of the biggest sources of inflammation in the body is poor dental health. Gums are often constantly inflamed in most people. See dental health for that. Otherwise, eat onions, grape leaves and seeds, yam, fennel, licorice, peony root, goldenrod leaves, and aspirin. Topically, apply chewed walnut husks, poplar stem bark, cottonwood bark, aspen bark, and black currant root bark. Pokeweed is toxic, but the tubers can be eaten, dried, or made into a topical application for inflammation. See also steroids.

Anti-seizure: There are no proven anti-seizure herbs. Except, traditionally cannabis was considered anti-seizure, but it may only be a muscle relaxer. However, some muscle relaxers may be anti-seizure too.

Muscle relaxers: Drugs like opiates and cannabis might be helpful.
Other muscle relaxers are cherry juice, chamomile, blueberries, and
cayenne. (Consume each, but chamomile may also be rubbed on.)
Eggs, fish, milk, almonds, beans, and brown rice have helpful
Vitamin D and Magnesium. Chamomile is made from daisies. Pick
the whole flower top and make into tea.

Blood pressure: If it is high, due to Dengue fever or other issue, try
a vasodilator. See Burdock and Hawthorne. Corn, garlic, and leeks
have mild effects. If it is medical treatment, you need one that is an
easily absorbed liquid or concentrated in a pill. Try chamomile tea
or peppermint tea or oil. Meditation is another way to reduce blood
pressure.

Antibiotics:

Antibiotics can easily be grown. Antibiotics are organism that eat
bacteria. Most antibiotics are viruses or fungi. There are thousands
of viruses in the soil and air. Most viruses are not harmful to
humans because viruses specialize in types of food to eat. Most
viruses eat bacteria. One of the earliest antibiotics was moldy
bread. Penicillin is one of many fungi that is common in the soil. It
becomes aerial and settles on food to spoil it. The pharmaceutical
industry takes up to twenty years to identify and test new medicines.
There are thousands of penicillin species identified, but only a small
number have been tested. However, if you are desperate for an
antibiotic, let bread or fruit go moldy and then try it on very ill
person. Mold is either eaten or rubbed on an infected part of the
skin. Certain diseases seem more susceptible to different strains of
penicillin. Either try it all or find one that works. After identifying
a beneficial strain, if you need a lot in a pandemic, you can plant it
on fresh bread to encourage that strain to grow. Since it is seeded, it
will outgrow other molds. To speed mold growth, keep the bread in
a warm, humid area. Under 1000 magnification with color staining,
the fungi look a little like a plant with a long stem and a few fronds
coming out of the top. Risks: Black mold are more likely toxic
than penicillin which is often white or blue. However, any mold
could be toxic, so you are taking a risk using it. Most common
symptoms of mold consumption are like seasonal allergies. Some
fungi cause diseases mentioned in this guide such as meningitis.

Mold requires moisture and warmth to grow. In humid summers,
mold grows faster on bread than in winter. Modern breads have
preservatives that slow mold growth, but still it will take time. Salt
is a preservative, so if you are making bread for the purpose of
mold, keep the salt out. Likewise, too much sugar, cinnamon or
vinegar might suppress mold. Most fruit bread will mold fastest.
Otherwise, keep bread moist by spraying or putting a moist paper
towel with it. Leave the bread out for an hour to get many mold
spores to land on it. Seal the bread. Keep it in a warm place, but
out of direct sunlight since UV light kills mold. A dark container
would be best to keep all light out. You may see mold grow in three
or four days. To make colonies of different antibiotics, divide each
spot into its own container with more bread. Despite looking the
same, they might each be different because there are thousands of
molds, but only a few colors. Each spot of mold will have fibers
growing through the bread beyond the extent of the spot.

In addition to bread, mold grows on other foods. Some mold is known to be bad such as the one growing on clover. However, you might look for mold in other foods such as fruits and take a chance if you are desperate.

Using mold has risks. People not being treated with it should avoid breathing it in, so process it outside. A very high quality mask or respirator might filter the mold. An allergic reaction to consuming an anti-biotic may be raised itchy red bumps. Allergic reactions usually occur instantly, but rarely can take hours to develop. The rash can be treated by steroids. You should also be prepared for GI symptoms. Bacteria can also grow on food. Also, using antibiotics hurts your gut microbiota. However, natural diets with lots of fiber and fermented foods are perfect for growing back the right microorganisms in your gut. Start with a small dose of your mold antibiotic, such as a large crumb, unless you are desperate.

Too many plants have anti-bacterial properties to list them all. This focuses on plants that are easily found. You should expect that plants have a milder antibiotic effect than penicillin molds. However, it takes time to grow penicillin so a plant may be a temporary solution. Hopefully, you find one below that is effective for your needs.

Purple loosestrife is a common invasive species in swamps. Other loosestrifes are not related, so don't try this with the other ones. Leaves and roots are antibiotic and said to be helpful with typhus. No severe side effects are known. Identification: Stems are square and red or purple. Flowers are reddish-purple and have six petals, but flower shape may vary.

Figure 15. Purple Loosestrife

Burdocks are plants that make large brown burrs that get stuck on clothing. Burdock burrs have hooked ends while thistles have straight. The lesser burdock has smaller leaves, and I suspect that the greater burdock has the same properties. The burr is collected when brown and saved. The seed is eaten as an antibiotic, but overdoses can cause low blood pressure, convulsions, and paralysis. No guidance on dosage is available. Be careful when separating seed from burr since burr is toxic and parts could be accidentally inhaled.

Horseradish is an antibiotic. Grind its roots. It is uncertain if the properties remain if cooked. Leaves can be used too. Too much is hazardous. Don't use for hepatitis. Look near streams for a plant with long leaves but shaped like dandelion, and flower clusters of small white flowers.

Silver Fir and Norway Spruce buds are antibiotic. Identify either as the ideal Christmas tree. Firs have short needles that are actually leaves. Base of needles are shaped like suction cups.

Asparagus seeds are antibiotic. Identification: When sprouting it is recognizable as the food. When fruiting it looks like tall dill with orange or red berries. The berries are mildly poisonous. Seed should be separated from berries. Asparagus causes sulfurous urine, and the poison acts on the kidneys, so smell of urine might be a gauge of toxicity levels.

Nutgrass tubers can be made into oil which is an antibiotic. Identification: It looks somewhat like grass that can grow tall except flower stems and seeds are different. Stems of flowers are triangular. The flower/fruit is spikelets. The tubers look like small nuts. The oil is edible and preferred.

Other plants are antibiotics. Try bottle gourd plant by extracting oil from seeds or using the fruit juice.

Antiviral: Try tea of bee balm or lemon balm leaves or shoots. Pregnant women shouldn't use this.

Antibiotics are usually consumed. Antiseptics are antibiotics applied to the skin. Resin of pine and fir trees is antiseptic. It is often made into turpentine oil by distillation first. The juice of onions and garlics is also antiseptic.

Pain management

See meditative pain relief. See production of aspirin. For headache pain, see that section. Few poppy plants produce enough opiate sap to be worth the effort of making it into an analgesic.

Willow can be made into salicylate acid, which is not identical to modern aspirin, but is related to it. All willows are genus Salix. Chew on bark or leaves or make tea from it. Salicylate acid comes from the sap, so eating sap should have the same effect. It will likely upset the stomach. Myrtle has been used as an alternative to willow.

You will need to try an amount of willow bark to determine the right dose. Watch for signs of overdose. Symptoms of nausea, vomiting, and dizziness may go away on own. Consider counteracting if there is a dramatic increase in ringing in ears, headache, fever, and irregular heartbeats. Aspirin overdoses can be treated with activated charcoal or baking soda to absorb any still in the stomach. You should hesitate to give aspirin for any disease that has head or brain inflammation because of a very small chance of Reye's syndrome. Examples of when to avoid aspirin if possible are flu, chickenpox, mumps ,or any viral infection. Symptoms of Reye's syndrome are similar to an overdose. It is a worsening of a headache, vomiting, and may turn into hyperventilation or hyperactivity. Removal of aspirin will improve most cases, but sometimes permanent brain damage is done. Risk levels reduce through puberty.

Topical anesthetics dull pain in a specific area. Cayenne peppers oddly cause pain in the mouth but dull pain topically. Try other peppers, too, since they all have the same capsaicin but in differing amounts. Also, all parts of the ginger plant can be used. Aspirin from willow bark can be used topically after leaching it from the bark. Also try Locust tree twigs and leaves.

For sore throats, consider aspirin, but see the warnings. Gargle with salt or sage leaf. Any type of sage should help. Maybe try chewing lilac leaves or bark. Steroids may help. Warm drinks plain or with honey, tea, mint, or distilled eucalyptus oil might help.

Major surgery or childbirth may require major pain management. Cannabis is dissociative, meaning that the patient will feel all the pain, but they won't care because it will feel like someone else is in pain. The whole plant can be used, but the leaves are mostly commonly used. There is a risk from any natural medicine, but the risks are generally higher with medicines that could knock someone out. All these medicines are defenses produced by the plant to kill whoever eats it. Therefore, proper dosage is imperative. No guidance is provided about effective doses. Additionally, pain management is often illegal, so check local jurisdictions. When administering, have a stimulant ready to counteract it, give the minimum dose and increase it if there is no effect, and then check for breathing and heartbeat. Try pawpaw seed, bark and seed of horse chestnut, coriander/cilantro seeds, poke weed root, eggplant leaves, a tea from the skin of honey locust fruit, and possibly lettuce sap. All parts of all poppies contain opium, but the opium poppy sap has the highest concentration. However, a cool climate may not encourage formation of the compounds. Dried sap of wild lettuces may have the same effect. Kidney bean root apparently has very high concentrations of narcotic. Yew is poisonous through narcotic action, and it only requires a very small dose. Use extreme caution with yew because reversing the effect with a stimulant will be difficult or impossible if the patient isn't awake to drink or is throwing up. Stimulants include okra seeds, spearmint, and fir tree resin. However, these stimulants may have mild effects and be unable to counteract the pain relief medication.

Figure 16. Yew.

Headaches: The two most common headaches are tension and migraines. Officially, no cause is known for migraines, but the author has it after eating certain processed foods. Others claim weather and fatigue are causes, but fatigue can be an initial symptom. Migraines may start as vision disruption starting small and progressing to a large patch of temporary blindness. Then an ache starts at the top of the head in a dome shape. To help with pain, analgesics or magnesium might help. Tension headaches are more common. Tension headaches can be felt as tightening or pain in any place in the head or neck. Tension headache may worsen until treated. Tension headaches can be caused by stress, anxiety, posture, or anything that causes wear on the head physically or mentally. Other causes include too little or too much sleep, so keeping a regular schedule is important. Analgesics such as ibuprofen help, but there are other cures. Tension headaches are most easily ended by non-medical means if the cure is implemented before the headache worsens. Since it is caused by mental and physical stress, removing that stress can help the headache. Meditation, discussed above, can instantly get rid of a small tension headache. Since tension headaches engage the head muscles, stretching them can relieve pain. To stretch neck muscles, first drop chin to chest and then slowly rotate side to side, second shrug shoulders, third put fingers on shoulders and make circles with elbows, and fourth move head side to side massaging shoulders on the lengthened side. Also, try specific head massages to relieve head tension. First try cupping hands over ears with fingers spread with static or rotating hands, and second try running your fingers slowly down your head starting at temples or forehead. Sinus headaches are at the front of the face, and stronger in mornings. Screen severe headaches as meningitis and stroke.

Kidney stones: The main issue with passing stones is pain management. However, kidney stones might be prevented or pass easier with apple cider vinegar, corn silks, and starch from reed roots.

Reproduction

Track 40 weeks of pregnancy since begging of last menstrual cycle. After 36 or 37 weeks, a baby will turn from head up to head down. If the mother-to-be is going into labor and the baby hasn't turned, you must try to help turn the baby. A breech delivery might go off okay, but it is better to try to turn the baby. After 38 weeks, turn the baby. The location of the large head and kicking feet can help you figure out the baby's location. Apply pressure to rotate it sideways. False labor is only a couple contractions within an hour, but no other signs. If the baby is near to full term and the mother's water breaks, then it is best to encourage delivery. To induce or aid delivery, see medical warnings below. Delivery is normally near when contractions are two minutes apart.

Healthy first time mothers tend to deliver late, so encouraging labor to start may be best. Avoid being more than two weeks overdue. Sexual intercourse especially when the woman has an orgasm can cause labor to start. The next level is to have a someone gently insert a finger and separate the amniotic sac from the uterus. A little more aggressive action is to break the amniotic sac.

Labor and delivery: Mostly you want to speed labor, so try walking. Mothers can deliver in almost any position. Squatting with support may ease delivery. Wash hands and remove jewelry, check for crowning, which is a visible head. Experts can check the cervix dilation to determine more accurately how far the baby is towards crowning. If the baby is crowning but still has the membrane of the amniotic sac, the pinch it to break it. Mothers will normally automatically push at the right time without being told to do it. As the baby's head comes, guide it. Never pull, but if it is shooting out too quickly, you may need to resist gently. Once you can see the nose, mouth, and neck, get the mother to stop pushing for a minute, clean out the baby's nose and mouth however you can, and then check to confirm the umbilical cord is not around the baby's neck. If it is around the neck, first try slipping around the head, but if that doesn't work it may turn out okay to deliver normally or to get the baby to slightly return in, so the cord is slack. Next, let the mother deliver. Hold on tight to the baby. The baby may turn to let the shoulders through. If there is trouble with shoulders, put pressure on the mother's abdomen. Wrap the baby and double check its health. The placenta normally comes out on its own after ten or fifteen minutes. The cord doesn't need to be cut at any particular time. Tie off and cut as close to the belly as possible. The vagina may have ripped. Suturing aids recovery. Many doctors make a cut before delivery to control where the rip occurs and to make it easy to suture. It may also ease delivery.

Cesarean sections are less common with women who are physically fit and who have practiced Kegel exercises. There are many benefits for women to practice Kegel exercises. Exercises are performed several times a day for several minutes by repetitively contracting and relaxing muscles of the pelvic floor. It can be practiced by starting and stopping urine flow but can be done at any time.

Cesarean section: This should be a last resort since major surgery has unknown consequences. Cardiac arrest of the mother is how bad it should be before attempting it without a complete medical setup and trained professionals. Pain killer is normally administered, but if the woman is in cardiac arrest, that may not be the main concern. It is better to cut straight across rather than up and down. Cut about three-quarters of the way across anywhere along the belly. Cut and pull back one layer at a time. If possible, stretch all muscles and blood vessels rather than cutting. Deliver the child. Clamp or tie, and cut the cord. Remove the placenta. Determine if a hysterectomy is necessary. If excessive bleeding is expected, a hysterectomy is advised. Suture the skin and any broken blood vessels. Revive the mother.

Birth control: Timing method: Women are fertile at a certain time of the menstrual cycle. Tracking that and deferring intercourse at that time may reduce pregnancies only 75% for typical people. However, the pregnancy rate can be as low as 5% if couple vigorously follow the rules. Problems include variation in women's cycles. Limit intercourse to after the 19th day of the cycle for a woman with a cycle length between 26 to 32 days. Also, track cervical secretions for viscosity changes that indicate fertility. Withdrawal: Removing before ejaculation may only reduce pregnancies by 75%. Lactation: When women breast feed, their chance of pregnancy reduces by about 90%. Vasectomy: Completely effective if done correctly but requires surgery. A vasectomy is a relatively easy surgery. Sanitize the scrotum. Apply pain killer if you have it because it can be as painful as any surgery. Plan your surgery if you haven't done one before by manual manipulation to locate the vas tubes taking sperm from testes upward. Cut into scrotum. Tie off both vas tubes going up into the vesicles in the body. You may also tie off them going down to the testes if desired. Then cut the vas tubes. Seal wound. Patient needs abstain for one week for healing. The first sex afterwards may contain sperm that was stored in the vesicles. Bruising is normal but watch for excessive ballooning indicating a failure of the tie offs. Intrauterine Device (IUD): An IUD is a T-shaped plastic device containing copper or hormones. It is placed in the uterus. The T-shape prevents it from coming out. Copper kills sperm. The success rate is 99% at preventing pregnancy. Bleeding may increase for a few months, but then should decrease. The T-shape is one and a quarter inch wide across the T, and two inches long. Copper can be in wire form, wound around the plastic. Condoms: Condoms were initially made from animal intestines or bladder and didn't necessarily cover the whole length but may have been tied with a ribbon. Some herbal medicines are said to either prevent fertilization, induce menopause, or change hormones to prevent ovulation, but risks are high, so use other methods.

For the health of the baby and mother the best separation of children is between three and a half and five years. However, after five years, there is only a slowly increasing risk for the mother (because of her age). Also, waiting at least two years limits most of the risks of pre-term birth. There is little risk in trying to have a child soon after a miscarriage that is early in term.

Preventing pre-term birth: Being in excellent physical, mental and dental health controls the risk factors for premature birth. Also avoid foods or medicines listed next.

Pregnant women shouldn't eat undercooked meat, but of course, no one should. Avoid organ meat, uncooked sprouts, alcohol, unpasteurized cheese, and smoked meats unless cooked before eating. Check the diet of pregnant women. Especially check folate, calcium and iron. However, overall, you want a balanced diet without an overdose in any vitamin.

Warnings on medicines: Most natural remedies have side effects. Some of them can influence reproduction including increasing risk of not carrying a fetus to term. Therefore, pregnant women should avoid these. Avoid anticoagulants (see stroke medicine section) because they increase bleeding. Most of anticoagulants are mild, so if eat, do so in moderation and balance with greens. Also avoid large doses of: aloe, chamomile, celery, beets, chard, thistle, nut grass, Queen Anne's lace, fennel, cedar, bee balm, marjoram, oregano, sorrel, poppy, sumac, blackberry, and chickweed. However, if a woman is overdue by a week, then it might be to the point of considering some of these to induce delivery. Birthing aides, including some that cause contractions should be avoided except in small quantities, such as parsley, sumac, currant, juniper, raspberry, yucca root and sedum. Strongly avoid cedar oil or juniper shoots. Avoid eating any food in excess because everything has some effects. Aspirin or any NSAID should be avoided in women late in pregnancy except at very small doses.

Excessive bleeding: Astringents constrict blood vessels. See Purple Loosestrife under the section on infections.

Baby care

Let the umbilical cord fall off on its own. It will dry faster if you don't get it wet when bathing the baby.

Diapers can be made from absorbent materials such as inner bark from cedar or silk from cattails. Alternatives are to use nothing, or leaves.

Nursing is good for baby and mother. There is no time limit to wean children, but they will eventually get bored of sitting still with mom. Milk from mammals may be a supplement or substitute, if necessary, but milk varies by animal, so it is not the perfect food for human babies. Cow's milk has more casein and less whey than human milk. Casein can be precipitated with vinegar, but then the milk will taste sour. Milk can be cup or spoon fed to an infant, but it will take longer. Porcelain bottles with spouts can be made but make the nozzle hole small so the baby has to suck. A wet nurse may be a better option when the mother can't nurse.

In winter, clothe the baby in one extra layer than you would yourself. In summer, clothe the baby the same as yourself. Clothes and bedding should always be in perfect condition so there is no strangulation risk.

There are tradeoffs for co-sleeping with baby versus putting in a crib. The biggest risk of co-sleeping is rolling onto the child. In any situation, be wary of strangulation risks. An infant wants to be in a relatively tight bassinette for the first few months. See basket making. It should be small enough that the baby can reach and touch both sides. Between four and twelve months, a crib is possible. A crib can be made the same as a bassinette but larger. A crib has many safety issues. A crib should have no large openings and nothing sticking out that clothing can get caught on. Bedding can be a suffocation risk if it is loose or has gaps. When a baby stands and walks, a low bed on the floor is best. Sleeping with adults or on the floor might be better than a crib since the only value of a crib is to control the baby and making it easier to reach them. An advantage to sharing a bed is that it is easier to soothe a baby back to sleep. There is less risk to the baby in co-sleeping as it gets older. All mattresses that babies sleep on should be firm. Co-sleeping is also a good method of birth control since it lowers intimacy between parents. Some cultures have a big age separation between children.

Baby food is produced with mastication. A care giver chews the food for the baby and then puts it in their mouth. To limit transmission of infection through saliva, this should be limited to close family.

Colic is unexplained crying. If it is unexplained, then there is little to say here about it. However, some mothers claim an improvement by simplifying her diet. If any person suddenly changes their diet, it takes time to adjust. It may take longer for babies to adjust since their digestive systems are immature.

Teething will begin sometime in the second half of their first year. Original pacifiers were made from carved bone. If you put a strap on it, make sure that it isn't a strangulation risk either because it is too short or because it is held loosely with a clip or pin. Nothing the baby can reach should be a choking risk. Nothing should be smaller than their throat size.

A list of a child's developmental milestones can be given, such as weight, height and social. However, the benefit of those is mostly diagnostic. Parents normally can figure out what the age-appropriate needs are for their children.

Skin

Warts: Half of warts go away in half a year, but if treatment is available, that is best. The sap of garden lettuce has been used to treat warts. Also consider any plant that produces latex like dandelions and milkweed.

Skin cancer: It will be red or black and often bleed. It will grow with time. Surgery is a common solution. It requires deep surgery to get the root.

Lotions: Natural oil produced by the skin is an ideal oil. If you wash excessively and need a body lotion, consider a food oil. Aloe can be used as a lotion, so see "burns" for instructions. Thorns from locust trees are anti-itch. Also, for itch, also try olive oil, sour dock root, ash of wheat plants, and some willow barks.

Sun protection: Loose, tightly-woven clothing filters the sun. Some natural products can have a very small protective effect. For example, some natural oils may improve protection 20%. Examples are olive, almond, and sesame oil and aloe.

Poison ivy's oil is in all parts of the plant. The ivy can be a vine or bush. It has leaves of three meaning three leaflets on the same leaf. Leaflets are smooth or notched. Yellowish-white flower clusters of small flowers appear from May to July. The fruit is off-white, clustered and appears August to November. Leaves distinctly red in fall. Plant often looks hairy (reddish). If touched, wash thoroughly with soapy cold water or rubbing alcohol. Antihistamines and corticosteroids help with symptoms, and they can be used for other rashes too. Poison sumac looks similar to staghorn sumac, but has white berries instead of tan, and poison stems are redder versus staghorn which is more rust hairy. Sumacs are bushes with oblong leaves. Poison oak is less common in the northeast US. Poison oak looks like oak leaves, but grows as a vine or bush, and the fruit is distinctly from an acorn but is small and greenish or yellowish balls.

Figure 17. Poison Ivy

Topical antifungals treat athletes' foot, jock itch and small red bumps on fingers. Try fruit of locust trees. Vagina or mouth thrushes can be treated by goldenrod leaves. Chewed columbine leaves or roots can be applied to ringworm which is a round fungal growth on the skin that looks like a red ring.

Topical anti-parasite: See columbine above. Try ground Pecan tree leaves. Wild greens or lettuces may work, but cultivated types are mild. Try juniper roots but see warnings for pregnant women. Try powdered cumin seed. Poison oak has been used, but the cure might be worse than the disease because it will make itching worse. Try ground up walnut husks.

Fingernails and toenails: Mothers can regularly bite the nails of their infants. Cut toenails straight across to avoid ingrown. That might be difficult to do once nails get old and hard. Soaking nails softens them. Rubbing them on a rough stone is one way to file them down.

Corns on the feet are due to poor footwear. Correcting the problem will make it go away. For pain, willow bark should help when applied to the skin.

Dental

In absence of premium dental care such as a water pick and sonic toothbrush, or a standard toothbrush and floss, other options can be found. You can make a toothbrush by fraying the end of a twig of a non-poisonous plant, such as a willow. As an alternative to toothpaste, ground, dried bark has been used from dogwood. The frays from the twig can also be used as a substitute for dental floss. The purpose is to remove food particles. If you are eating acidic food wait for the acid to decrease in your mouth before brushing. Fibrous vegetables and dairy product increase saliva which helps protect teeth. Massaging gums with fingers may help, too. Gum can be helpful in cleaning teeth if it is not too sticky to teeth. Gum can come from edible tree bark, roots, leaves, nuts, or sap. Sugar pine and spruce are two trees know for gum from sap. Sap can be extracted by making zig-zag gashes in the bark but may take reduction to make it the right thickness. When yellow-gray plaque builds up, it should be removed by a dental hygienist. They use tools to remove it through scaling above and below the gum lines. It is important to remove all plaque so special shaped tools are necessary to get the whole tooth surface. Tartar (calculus) is plaque that is hardened and may require more aggressive tools and effort.

Fluoride naturally occurs in groundwater but may be below needed levels. It is most common where surface soils are igneous rocks. It is found in higher levels in groundwater in the southwest US (California, New Mexico, Arizona, Nevada), and parts of Utah and Oregon. The Great Lakes have a moderate amount. The only other higher place in North America is in the Mexican State of Chihuahua. No high areas are found in Europe. The lethal dose of Fluoride is about one thousand times what is found in a serving of toothpaste. The first symptom of excessive fluoride is likely to be gastrointestinal discomfort. Long-term overuse may make teeth have white patches or become stained. Mixing with rainwater might give you the right dose in the highest areas. Grapes may have it. The tea plant draws fluoride from the ground. Tea plants are shrubs that can be grown in Marine environments that don't get colder than -12 Celsius or 10 Fahrenheit and that are somewhat wet.

Chewing on nut grass tubers prevents cavities. See identification with antibiotics. Chewing on walnut tree bark or green husks reduces tooth pain.

Pulling teeth: At some point you will need to pull teeth. The purpose of wisdom teeth is to fill in the gaps where other teeth have fallen out, so either you will have to pull unneeded wisdom teeth, or other ones to make room for them. Wisdom teeth should be pulled when they start to cause pain or crowd the other teeth. Other teeth should be pulled if they cause pain that can't be remedied by dental work. If dental care has been poor, simply grabbing the tooth, wiggling, and pulling with thumb and finger may be enough to get it out. Specially shaped pliers are helpful if some leverage is necessary. Bleeding will occur. Use gauze to stop bleeding. Also, rinse with warm salt water but do not spit, which risks dislodging the blood clot while healing.

Dentures or false teeth: To create a model of what needs to be created, use bees wax. Teeth can be made from wood, other teeth, animal bone, easily carved rocks, ivory, animal horn or porcelain. To hold in place in the mouth, either make wider than required for a tight fit, or tie with a gold band.

Teeth grinding relief: Symptoms include increased pain in many teeth, loosening of teeth, and a pattern of wear across crowns of teeth. Early diagnosis could be from family members that listen for tapping of teeth. Grinding teeth while sleeping may be due to stress and other factors. Grinding teeth while awake is more clearly associated with stress and is something that can be consciously controlled with concentration. Deal with the stress. The treatment is to use a bite splint to keep teeth apart and possibly hold them tight. Dental guards can be made from bone. The guard doesn't need to fit precisely in order to prevent future damage, but the tighter the fit, the better it will be for getting teeth to tighten in their place. You goal is to make it one-eight inch thick. You want to be able to close the mouth. Also, you don't want to make the tongue move from its natural position. One way to make it is to repetitively try it. You could put something soft, like gum on the surface so you can see where the teeth are indenting on it. Alternatively, you could use gum to mold around the teeth so you can see their shapes.

Straightening teeth with dental braces is almost always motivated by cosmetic reasons. However, straight teeth can help with efficient chewing. Teeth need to move very slowly so they aren't forced out of their sockets. A dental guard could be repeatedly modified to slowly move teeth. Catgut has been used to tie between teeth to move them. See suturing in trauma for catgut.

Mental health

Just as personalities vary, inclinations to various psychological difference exist. Sometimes the inclination so strong that you can do little to prevent it deepening into a psychological disorder. Some children are more prone to anxiety, depression, etc. The human brain becomes more fixed after the teen years. A child with problems doesn't always end up being an adult with problems. However, a child with different needs should be taken as someone that needs help to avoid later problems. For example, you should be able to tell early how prone your child is to anxiety. Adjust all of your parenting to fit. While an anxious child is young, exposure to many situations will help them be less anxious to new things later. However, always be cautious and do only what they are ready to do.

General methods to limit stress: meditation, talking about feelings, writing about feelings. Many men only share feelings with their significant other, so being in a relationship is good for men's mental and physical health.

Human differences exist. If a person's behavior doesn't harm them or others, it is best for their mental health to accept their difference.

During an anxiety attack: Breathe in for 5-10 seconds. Breathe out for 5-10 seconds. Repeat for two to three minutes. Optional: close eyes, listen to your breathing, breathe in through nose and out through mouth. Then talk about the feelings that caused the attack.

Emotional trauma happens. If it is expected, such as the death of a loved one, talk through it in advance. Whatever positive coping skills you use, such as religious faith, can be learned by those around you. After an unexpected trauma, emotional demands may be higher since it is sudden. Let people grieve but be prepared with coping mechanisms. Don't offer coping mechanisms too soon so they can grieve properly. Post-traumatic stress disorder (PTSD) most commonly happens after trauma, especially if it is near bedtime. If someone attempts to go to sleep while still in shock it will solidify the trauma as PTSD. Don't let someone sleep that is traumatized unless their health is otherwise compromised.

Treatment:

Counseling goals are to get the person to talk and change. Cognitive therapy is talking through things. Behavioral therapy is getting patients to change their behaviors. CBT is both. CBT is more likely to work on mild problems.

Psilocybin or magic mushrooms are illegal in most developed countries and are not recommended. Psilocybin is actual a group of mushrooms in the same family that appear about the same. The mushrooms appear throughout the world. Identification: They all have caps above ground on stalks. Under the cap, they have gills, brown spores. They are usually small and tan to brown in color. Otherwise, an experienced person could sample one to see if it produces the right effect. See alkaloid poisoning if you consume the wrong type. A typical dose is 2 grams of dried psilocybin, which is less than one average mushroom. Two grams is equal to the weight of 2 cubic centimeters of water. Treatment with psilocybin is effective for anxiety, depression, and bipolar disorder. Research on treatment has followed this methodology: A few counseling appointments are conducted to set the specific goals for treatment and to develop trust between counselor and patient. The treatment may last a whole day or more after one dose of psilocybin. When the psilocybin takes effect, expect the patient to need emotional support. It is important for the patient to be comforted. The counselor will guide the patient through normal counseling while dosed. Afterwards, follow up counseling should be done. A single treatment is likely to last at least half a year. Psilocybin is not known to be addictive. Other hallucinogens may have a similar effect. For example, raw day lily leaves are hallucinogen, but you may need to eat a lot. Unripe mulberries are too.

Alcohol, chamomile, and cannabis are often used by people with anxiety. However, relief is temporary, and using them can be addictive. The threshold for addiction is daily use. Multiple sclerosis, Alzheimer's disease and Parkinson's disease are neurological diseases that can cause anxiety and are more likely in older people. This type of anxiety can be relieved by cannabis.

Foods containing magnesium, such as pigweed grain, reduce biological causes of anxiety.

Crafts

Craft doesn't mean hobbies in this case, but the result of skilled work. Goods are no longer manufactured but crafted. Crafts might be used for any purpose. A glue might be made to make a tool, such as an arrow, and then used for hunting for protection. Clay might be necessary for water filtration or pot making for pleasure, as a lamp or for storage.

Clay is the finest (smallest) soil particles can be. (Large particles are gravel and sand.) All flat areas of ground are likely to be made from soil deposits, and often because of settlement in water. Clay deposits occur where the water was running the slowest, so small particles settled. Even in mountains, you can find clay in former lake beds. However, clay is often mixed with other soil particles. To filter out the clay, you can mix the soil in water and then wait for it to settle in layers. Clay is lighter than sand so will be above it. Some clays are expansive which means they swell too much in water. Volcanic clays are more likely to be expansive. Do a test of drying the clay to see how much it cracks.

Clay pots or bricks are much stronger if fired. (Bricks are best when mostly sand, and then clay plus lime if you have it. See the rocks section.) Drying bricks will give them some strength and durability, but firing is best. Hotter is usually better in a kiln since it converts it from earthenware to stoneware to porcelain. Raise and then lower the temperature slowly. Kilns are enclosed for several reasons: enclosed fires can get hotter and keep the heat. Clay pots don't weather well in freezing conditions. Glazing protects the earthenware by making it less porous. Common basic glazes can be made from salt or ash. Ash is improved with lime. Ash should be completely burned and sieved. Ash is less harmful if you leach the lye from it before use. Any salt may be used, but it works better with higher iron in the salt or clay. Put a salt mixture with water in the kiln once it is very hot, then it will vaporize to steam. You want the temperature to be much higher than the boiling point before adding salt water so that the chemical reaction will take place and you are not just boiling off water.

Brooms: A tree branch will work. To make a more effective one, start with a round broom by bundling straw around a branch. Sorghum was the most effective material, but any fiber can work if it is durable. To make a flat broom, you would need a vise to hold the fibers.

Stone hand axes are often made from flint or chert, but any rock that fractures correctly may work. Use a hand axe to dig, butcher animals, as a weapon, or to chop wood or remove tree bark. Flint or chert are crystalline rocks found around limestone or sedimentary deposits. You want to select a rock that will break easily along sharp edges, but not shatter like volcanic glass might. The size and shape can vary based on purpose. Generally, they are triangular or oval and sized so the larger half fits in the hand with the pointed end sticking out. Use a hard stone like a cobble to hit the source stone to get it generally in an axe shape. Then use finer work to get the exact shape. An antler (not bone) or piece of wood might work for this. The point is made by applying pressure to the parts needing removal. A pointed edge is better for scraping. A long, thin piece can be fit to a wood handle to make a knife. Save the flakes to use for arrowheads, spearheads, needles, or fire-starting flint. To cut larger branches or trees with a hand axe, use it like a chisel and strike it with another object. Attaching a handle wasn't done until the bronze age but could be attempted with a stone axe. A stone may not be able to handle the higher stress from swung impact. However, oblong stones were attached to handles to be hammers.

Combs: Make from fine grained wood such as cherry.

Glue: Tree (pine and spruce) resin can be a simple, ready glue. Birch bark can be made into glue by burning the bark in open air near a smooth vertical surface like a large stone. The smoke will collect on the stone. Don't expect much volume of glue. Scrape it from the rock. It tends to weather poorly and be brittle. See bitumen cement as an alternative. Animal glue can be made from most animal parts but is made mostly from skin and bones because they are often waste. Break down the tissue with lime, rinse off the lime and treat with acid to neutralize, and then heat in water at slowly increasing temperatures while drawing off water and adding more once it starts to produce glue at around 158 degrees. Hide glue is sensitive to being too warm. Glue can also be made from starch and acacia.

Plastic: Edible wax is discussed related to food. Harden it further to make plastic. Modern commercial plastic is made from crude oil. Each plastic is identified by a code and behaves differently. One reason that it is very hard to recycle plastic is that when plastic reaches a certain temperature, it degrades. Plastic is long chains of molecules and if they break in high temperatures, cooling may make it solid, but not weaker than before. It you try to melt commercial plastic with recycling codes 3, 6, and 7, you will probably produce toxic gas. Code 7 is a grouping of miscellaneous so may vary in quality. Latex from plants such as milkweed sap can be made into rubber. Hypothetically, it could be used like chewing gum. Latex naturally coagulates into low quality rubber with time. Natural rubber will be sticky in hot situations. To vulcanize rubber to make it harder, usually sulfur and heat are added. Sulfur is found near hot springs, volcanoes or in gypsum.

Lubricating oil: You can make birch oil from birch bark by heating the birch in a fire. Heat the bark in an inflammable container where the oil can drip into a container below it.

Microscopes: anything that bends light can be used as a microscope. An example is a drop of water, a gem, or the point of a needle.

Useful rocks: Coal is shiny, black and in sedimentary bands. Salts are usually in dry lake beds and are light colored and translucent. Sulfur is yellow, found near volcanoes or thermal hot pots. Lime is very common. Lime is from seabed deposits. Most of the world was under water at some point, so you have a good chance of finding limestone. Limestone is a soft, light gray sedimentary rock. You should be able to easily make it into a powder between two rocks. Fossilized shells might be harder to crush. Limestone also dissolves relatively easily compared to other rocks. See also the section on locating ore. Iodine is very rare and hard to process. Iodine is slightly higher in a rare form of limestone, caliche, and is extracted through a multi-step process using sulfate and chlorine or potassium.

Baskets can be made from leaves of reeds, nut grass, day lily, or bulrush. Baskets are for carrying or storage. Baskets can also be used to trap small animals. For a more durable basket, use willow branches or vines. Wood and branches are softer if soaked first.

Acids: Vinegar can be made by the slow fermentation processes above. Distilled vinegar is not vinegar that has been distilled, but made from pure or distilled alcohol. To speed vinegar formation in other sources, add a mother or lees which is a the bacteria leftovers from previous fermentation, and a source of oxygen such as alcohol. Distilled vinegar is usually five percent acid and has a pH of 2.6.

Bases/Alkali: Limestone is a primary source of lime which is a base. Quicklime is a superior form of lime. Burning lime at above 825 degrees C or 1517 degrees F converts it to quicklime. It will reduce in volume by a third or more. Either use quicklime soon, store it in an air tight container, or slack it with (mix in) water. Adding water will increase the volume significantly, up to triple in size. Lye is another base. See above for making lye from wood ash.

Cloth

Clothing is a form of shelter.

To tan hides into leather: spread it out and scrape everything off it you can, cover with salt (mineral salt is fine, also lime), dry for a couple days. It should feel hard at this point. Remove salt and soak in water until completely soft. Wring dry. Mix egg yolk and water (one yolk to half a cup of water.) (An alternative to egg yolks is animal brain with a little bit of added fat. Another is tannin leached from tree bark.) Rub in the yolk solution, and then stretch the leather in every direction. Experience will help you determine how much stretch each hide can take before tearing. Keep stretching until completely dry. Drying can be quickened with heat. If it ends up hard, you can repeat the egg, stretch and drying. Lastly, smoke the hide like meat.

Thread for sewing, string, twine, yarn or cordage/rope: First choose a fiber. Thread: Common fiber sources for thread are cotton, sheep's wool, jute, milkweed, hemp, and leaves of yucca. Second, make the source into fibers. Third, spin it into thread. With a lot of thread, and a loom, fabric can be woven. Try lots of natural fibers and bark. Thicker thread can be made from strips of leather. Thinner thread can be made from tendons (sinew) of large animals where the meat might be too tough to eat. To spin cordage: start near middle of a strand of fiber, but not the exact middle. Spin with fingers at that point until kinks, spin one side and then spin both sides around each other, repeat, and then when nearing end splice in another piece by laying it over the other piece where each fiber goes with the other one, then tie off the end.

A hand loom can be made to make fabric. However, a thicker fabric such as for rugs makes more sense from a labor standpoint than fine clothing. A simple hand loom is just a wooden frame. Strands are tied in one direction. Fibers are fed through in the other direction alternating over and under the strands.

Water pouches can be made from leather. After sewing to make a container, pour in something hard like a hard grain to stretch it to shape. Leather should be soaked and then force the grain in. Leather will leak, so it needs to be sealed with a wax such as hot beeswax. Seal outside and inside. You will need a tight stopper made from a branch of a tree. Use a softer wood that produces edible foods. Gourds can be used to make water bottles. Pick a gourd that is stable, so you don't spill. Sand off the outside, saw off top, shake out, seal with wax on inside and out, and make a cork from poplar or fir trees. Pitch could seal the outside, but may taste bad on inside.

Bleaching: Bleach is often produced from salt. Chlorine is dangerous and has been used as a chemical weapon. Production of chlorine requires very high amounts of electricity and complicated membrane cells. Rely instead on substitutes such as UV light for water sanitation and removing colors. To dye clothes, almost every plant has can be used as a dye.

Gloves: If you have made knitting thread from wool or other fur, you could knit or crochet mittens or gloves. The thicker the thread, the easier it will be to make a mitten quickly. However, thick mittens aren't good for summer work. Leather can be made thin and flexible. You would have to seal it, so it doesn't absorb water and harden. You can thin leather or split it to make it the right thickness. Make a template by either using an existing glove, or through measurement. A glove can be made with two pieces but fits better when made with more. A glove with two pieces might be satisfactory for some work tasks when the hands don't need full coverage such as preventing blisters. Additional pieces can go along the finger, go around the tip, and come down the other side. The seams are normally abutted together and sewn with a fine thread.

Footwear: Shoes are sometimes not thought as necessary, but that was before understanding of infectious diseases. See discussions of tetanus in the section on infections. Early forms of footwear include a leather bag. Leather is sewn closed along the top of the shoe in a seam. Lacing can pull it closed over the food. An improvement is to sew upper and lower pieces together to make a moccasin. Sandals were another early type of footwear. Sometimes they were made with cordage from reed, willow, or palm leaves. The thick cordage formed the shape of the sandal and provided some cushion. Other cordage was used to tie it into shape. The straps were also cordage, and could be a simple V or thong, but an improvement is to have a strap around the ankle. A wooden clog was made when more protection was needed. Clogs can be worn over leather moccasins and may just be a board with a strap. Since clogs do not bend, the front was often curved up so the foot could rotate more naturally while walking. A clog is carved, so soft wood will make it easier. Keep the clog dry to improve its life. More advanced shoes, sandals or boots can be made by sewing leather pieces together. Leather can be varying thickness from various animals based on need. The sole of the shoe should be thick and durable, but the uppers should be softer. The sole was cut from the thickest part of cow hides. Boots were initially separate pieces that became protected. Leggings can be worn when the area above the shoe needs protection.

Insulation of gloves and footwear could be done like bedding (below). Alternatively, use leaves of reeds, or sunflowers, bark of some trees that is hairy, or milkweed seeds.

Bedding can be made from any material. Fur can be very warm in winter, and leather can be cooling in summer. Fur is leather where the hair has been left on. For padding of cushions, pillow, or bedding, consider goose down if you want insulation. Many birds have an insulating layer under their flight feathers. Other fillers are wool, cotton, straw, or buckwheat.

Lighting

Candle wicks are preferred to be cotton but are often treated with fire retardant to slow them from burning too quickly. Any natural material such as milkweed seed floss could be a wick. It needs be able to draw melted wax up through capillary action, so braided fabric is preferred. Treatments of wicks include salt and borax which are dissolved in water, and then the wicks are soaked in them. Borax is a salt found on shores of evaporating lakes. Something to try is to put wicks in a container of seawater and let it evaporate. (I don't know if these things have ever been tried.) See wax under food.

Oil lamps come in many designs. A simple lamp can be made from clay pottery, a wick and oil. See candle wicks above. The minimum requirements are that it have a place for oil and a way to hold a wick such as a nozzle. Other design features are handles, enclosing the oil vessel with a top to prevent spillage, and multiple nozzles. Oil used includes food oils and animal fats. An advantage over candles is that the oil doesn't have to be converted to wax and formed into a candle shape. A disadvantage of lamps over candles is that the wick needs to be manually advanced. A stick can be used to push the wick from the back end.

Writing

Ink: Soot from oil lamps can be used. If the ink is a dry formulation, a wet brush can lift it. Other pigments: iron, colorful clay, burned bones, and animal hide. Good liquids are solvents such as turpentine that dissolve the colorant and evaporate quickly once on paper. There are few ways to make ink otherwise such as boiling staghorn sumac fruit and leaves.

Pens: An ink pen can be made from a bird's feathers. Also, reeds can be used. Reeds can have a small slit that acts as a reservoir for liquid ink. Soaking the pen will keep it from cracking when made.

Pencils: A singed twig or branch may be a suitable pencil. Other pencil leads are the elements of silver and lead. A silver or lead stick can be held and sharpened through grinding to a point. The hard graphite in modern pencils is rarer than lead and silver. Powdered graphite can be compacted with a clay binder into a lead.

Paper: White bark from birch trees might satisfy a need. Fibers used are wood pulp, hemp, papyrus (white inner stem of the reed plant). Parchment is untanned leather and used similarly to paper. Make parchment by scraping and drying skins under tension. To make paper from fiber, collect the fiber, beat to a pulp, bleach if necessary, use a fine cloth to screen out pulp from a bath, drain until the coating is on the fabric, and then put in a press to extract water and dry it. Clay tablets are a crude option.

Electronics

You can operate some electronic devices by linking AAA, AA, C, or D batteries together. You will need the correct voltage and current (amps). All common batteries are 1.5 volts. A laptop commonly uses 20 volts, so that means you would need 13 or 14 batteries end to end to get the voltage. To get the current (amperage), it depends on the size of batteries in your improvised power supply. Unlike combining batteries end-to-end, putting batteries side by side usually doesn't work because they need to be exactly matched. It is better to have one battery across the width but try them in parallel if there are no other options. Laptops need around 5 amps which is about right for a C battery. For charging a USB device, cut the USB cable and split it to get leads to put on a battery. For most USB charging devices, 5 volts and AA or AAA is good, but some hardware needs 20 volts and higher amps. USB wire: red or orange is positive, and black or blue is negative.

Electronics can last for a very long time. The most common problems that reduce the life of electronics are corrosion, short circuits, button failures, and wear. Corrosion can come from water, if it is a washer, but battery corrosion is a major cause. If you have battery devices, remove the batteries when not in use, or inspect regularly. Mild corrosion can be cleaned with alcohol, or water and vinegar or baking soda. Some short circuits may be from build-up of conductive dust. Clean exposed circuitry regularly. If a circuit has been overloaded and electrical damage has been done, if you can't see the damage, with extensive effort, individual components can be tested. Button failures are often wear failure of the exposed false button, so remove the external button to expose the electronic switch. Identify wear before it becomes severe to prevent failure.

Rechargeable batteries come with many chemistries such as lithium, lead-acid, and nickel-cadmium. They vary in their ability to hold charges, but don't rely upon any to hold charges for a long time. They should be for temporary storage of power, or to make power portable. The rule of thumb is that most rechargeable batteries lose their ability to hold charge so that after 10 years, they are much less capable than at the beginning. Other means of energy storage are to store electricity in capacitors for a very short time, or to store a mass such as water at a height and then use it later to drive power system. A lead acid battery is terminals of lead sulfate which is lead oxide treated with warm sulfuric acid, and liquid between the terminals is sulfuric acid diluted in water.

Solar arrays produce DC current which is either stored in batteries which are DC, or it is inverted to AC and connected to the grid. After power comes out of batteries, it is inverted before it goes into the grid. To get a solar power system to work when everything is out, you need to disconnect from the grid. DC could be used to directly charge batteries for cars or accessories, but it may be easiest to go through the inverter and then the charger because that will control the current flow. If you have a battery, the systems should control delivery of however much power you need until it runs out. Batteries will be capable of delivering the maximum when you turn them on but will diminish until they are at a low level. Without batteries, or if they are old, you would have to exactly match the power being produced. If a cloud comes, you will have a brownout. At some point, batteries will not hold a charge, so should be removed from the system. Some types of energy use can be done during the day. Your priorities for energy use may be tools, water pumps, and dental hygiene. In summer, you may want fans, and in winter, heat distribution systems. Farming equipment or milling and grinding equipment. Lighting is nice but requires batteries.

Transportation

Horses can be used for riding, pulling buggies, and pulling plows. Some breeds are better at each, but one horse can do many things. They are a lot of work to train, feed, and care for. Care: Horses need shelter. They will want room to roam when not working. Hooves should be cleaned. Shoes or hoof boots are necessary if walking on hard ground or if they work hard. Keep horses' feet dry. Horses aren't livestock, but service animals, so have high value. Therefore, they may need the same medical and dental care that humans need. Feed: Horses will eat grasses but prefer oats and vegetables. It will need salt unless soil and plants provide it. It will eat about two percent of its weight each day. It can work harder if it has grain instead of only grass. Don't abruptly change feed. It will drink ten gallons of water a day. Training: Wild horses and foals need training. An adult horse will forget its training if not regularly reinforced. Part of training is handling equipment such as buggies and plows. A large part of training is to desensitize the horse to stimuli. Horse personalities tend to be very flighty. Horse breaking and horse whispering are opposing views. A horse can be gently coaxed by slowly increasing the stimuli. That doesn't necessarily mean leaving and returning over several days but can be slowly adding and removing the stimuli in greater depth over a single day.

Scooters and bicycles: It is difficult to make a bicycle without modern manufacturing methods. The hardest part is the gear and chain. Earlier bicycles had the pedals directly on the front wheel. A scooter that is stood on or sat on is another option. A scooter is propelled by kicking. Scooters have no suspension, so riding on flat even ground is best. A wood scooter can be made. The axle needs to be thick unless it can be metal. Use the most durable woods. Rubber tread is another possible improvement. Wheels can be solid, but also see wagon wheels.

Wagon wheels: Draw a template for end and side views. If you have car wheels use them. The hub (center) is best made with a lathe. To make it fit, being perfectly center may not be necessary, but to make the wheel balanced, you should make the hub and all parts as even as possible. When putting in spokes, make longer than needed, glue in place, then cut to exact length needed. (Spokes go

to outside of the rim.) The rim segments span two rim spokes.
Rims can be cut from one thick board. Make one rim larger than
needed so after fitting the rims together, the last one will fit without
gap. The joints between rims need to be jointed with an extra piece.
Wagon wheels sometimes had a steel band that was heated until
expanded just enough to fit over the rims. Without the band, you
have less durability. Alternatively, a sacrificial wear layer could be
adhered. The layer could be a thin board bent around and glued on.

Some dogs have been trained to pull carts. Large, husky dogs, such
as St. Bernards can pull loads. Sled dogs also are used to pulling.

Building construction

Consider the placement of a building in relation to landscaping.
Trees and ground are important. Winds from the south usually
bring warm air, and wind from the north bring cold. In the north,
the philosophy is to block wind from the north, but allow it from the
south. Despite wind from the south being warm in summer,
windchill is all the cooling that you will get. Staying warm in
winter is more important in the winter, so block the north wind.
This often done by putting evergreen trees on the north side, and tall
leafed shade trees on the south side of a building. The shade trees
will lose their leaves in winter, so you get solar heating then. A
building that is shaded can stay very cool. If you only open the
windows at night, and there is no sun on the building and no internal
sources of heat, then it will be coolest. Vines will shade a building
but will destroy roofing. Short temporary sun shade like sunflowers
is helpful, too. The ground should slope away from the building on
all sides to get water to drain.

Foundations: Put foundations below the frost line unless the whole
structure is light and can float on the soil. Frost lines are four to
five feet in the most northern US States. It decreases by about one
foot per state south of there. If the foundation will ever see water,
then a cement or stone foundation is best. A little cement will help
keep the stones in place if there is every shifting. Cement is limes
and clays that have been heated to thousands of degrees and ground.
Alternatives to cement are bitumen which is natural asphalt, burnt
gypsum with some sand, and lime from crushed oyster shells with
or without volcanic ash. If you are able to calculate the weight of
your structure plus contents, you should plan that the soil can hold
at least one thousand pounds per square foot of foundation area but
can be much higher. An exception is peat, which is formerly

wetlands, and will hold less. Also, sand can hold heavy loads if it is deep and compacted, but not if it is loose at the surface. A posthole filled with concrete might give you enough strength for a lightweight structure. To keep termites and carpenter ants away from wood construction, either extend the foundation above ground by a foot, or try to use cedar near the ground. A sheet metal shield also helps. Keep vegetation away from the base of your foundation so you can inspect it for insects.

Bricks: Stone cobbles can be bricks, but you can make them too. The best ratio of materials is two parts sand to one-part clay. The clay you find may already have some sand in it. If you have some lime, add it to increase the strength of the brick. Plant fiber and waste oil may also increase strength. Also, sometimes iron ore or rust is added. You need enough water to moisten the materials but how much depends on the shaping method. For mud brick, place into form and then let dry. You can increase the strength by compacting the brick. The best clay brick is one that is fired in a kiln at 1000 degrees, but any heat likely helps. Dry the bricks before heating. Mortar between bricks can be the same mixture as the brick. It will be slightly weaker, but that is normally good for brick recycling later.

Sod homes: Cut sod two by one foot and half a foot deep. Pile to make walls. Leave openings for doors and windows and use the same methods for them as other types of construction. Use the same methods for roofing as other construction. For sod homes, water is an even more important concern because it can cause erosion of sod. A sod home is quick to build if you have a plow but takes maintenance to keep in shape if water isn't controlled. Sometimes the outside of a sod home was plastered.

Wood construction:

Among wood structures, log cabins require the most total amount of materials, but the least total effort and least sophisticated tools among wood methods. However, thick heavy logs can require a few strong people to lift, especially when working at heights. Straight pine and spruce are preferred. Pick trees that are the same size. Remove the bark. Either use the full rounded tree cross-section or square off. You should easily be able to estimate how many trees you need based on trunk widths and stacking them. Start with a stone foundation. Flooring can be earth, stone, or floorboards. If putting floorboards on the ground, then they will be at the level of the bottom half of the first log. If putting elevated floorboards, you will have to slot them into a log at their ends. Use mud to seal between layers. At ends, logs will lap so that alternating layers are half a layer higher than the previous layer in the other direction. (Think of Lincoln Log toys.) At corners, slot the logs by cutting each to one quarter of its width on each side for the log above and below. Measurements of intersecting log width will help get the slot the right size, but you may lift and try it a few times to get it right. One log goes the whole length of the structure unless you have an opening. Interior walls could be made of logs that intersect mid-length on the exterior wall logs. Otherwise, there are no interior walls, or they are made with other construction methods. Likewise, openings could have the same corner design, but often a vertical slot is made in their ends at openings to insert a piece to hold them together. Roofs can be logs if heavy loads are expected or if ease of construction is desired. At two ends, the logs continue up in a V-shape, unless other construction methods are transitioned to here. The roof holds the gables from tipping over. For purlin design, logs going between gables tie them together and support the roof. One ridge beam is required at the top. The spacing between the purlin ties and ridge beam depends on the weight of roof, shingles and snow, and the strength of sloping roofing boards or logs. With logs, you may not need purlins. Other options are to transition to post and beam or framing balloon in the roof.

Post and beam timber construction uses squared-off logs for vertical support columns, and horizontal beams. This requires a medium amount of materials and skill. Wind in log homes was carried by friction between logs, but for post and beam, wind needs consideration. Framing a structure into a box shape with posts and beams would provide no resistance to wind. The most common way of resisting the wind with post and beam construction is to put diagonal brace logs. Sometimes they are at each corner, but sometimes they cross from corner to corner of an opening. Alternatively, filler material such as brick or stone can provide resistance. Post and beam construction requires siding or filler material. Also, see wind resistance in framing balloons. Connecting timbers together requires more effort, so see woodworking below. Construction can transition between methods at the level of the roof. However, most commonly, there are ridge beams and close purlins to hold sloped roof boards.

Balloon-Framing requires the most skill and tools, but the lowest amount of materials. Technical or design skill is required too. Just as how post and beam construction considered more thought for wind, balloon-framing requires consideration of many more things. Wind is often carried in complicated arrangements of wallboard and collectors. Roofs are often constructed from trusses and sloping rafters. Even if you have skills and tools, you need to locate or produce stick lumber and nails. This is beyond what can be described here.

Siding: The primary purpose of siding is to keep the weather out of the walls. However, for balloon-framing, wall board keeps the building from blowing over in wind. Stone and brick can be siding, but it is best to use a double layer of materials with an air gap in between. Water will seep through stone mortar and brick, so a gap will cause the water to go down instead of in. The inner layer could be wall board. You may need a triple wall if you want to insulate too and have only loose insulation. Siding can be shingles. See below. Clapboards are essentially wide wood shingles but are rotated so the vertical tree grain goes sideways.

Shingles: When shingling, start at the bottom and work up. Shingles should overlap so that water will flow off one shingle onto the one below. Use the minimum number of nails or other fasteners so that shingles can thermally expand and contract. Keep the fasteners on the top half so the holes they make will stay dry. Also leave gaps side to side for expansion. Wood shingles or shakes are best from cedar since it is durable. Other choices are redwoods, pine, and spruce. Shakes are split. The length depends on skill, but two feet is common. Widths are half a foot but depend on skill. Thicknesses vary from thin to up to an inch thick. Slate tiles are broken from rock. They are attached through a hole drilled for a peg. Clay roof tiles should be made into shapes based on their purpose. Some time is flat like slate. Other clay tile is alternating pieces sideways that are flat and curved which allows for less vertical overlap. An alternative is two curved pieces alternating curvature direction. Asphalt shingles are very common. They can be made with a fabric such as cotton, felt, jute or wood pulp. The sealant is bitumen. Asphalt shingles may come in any size including rolls. When large rolls are used, it is attached by torching the underside, so it sticks. Sand on the top is optional. Thatch roofs can be made of reeds, straw, rush, palm, or sedge. Thatch should be densely packed so that it is impenetrable to water. Small bundles are made on the ground. See cordage for options, but also consider hazel sticks. Thatch may be built up over years as lower levels weather if it is straw, but reed is more likely replaced fresh. Thatch can last as long as other roofing options if on a steep roof and done well. Aim for a 50-degree roof slope with thatch. In areas with snowfall, the support should be stronger and closer for thatch. Fire risk is significant with thatch, so be careful of ash from cooking and heating landing on the roof. Consider other forms of heat and cook away from the structure. Otherwise, chimneys should be extra tall, and fuels should be chosen based on whether they produce ash. The method of installation can vary by thatch type. Some materials require doubling up. Overlap is at least half of the length of the bundles. For fastening, see nails or dowel wood construction. Recycling of asphalt shingles may not work because the shingles self-seal to one another. However, you could attempt careful removal from the top by pulling the nail first and then trying to break the seal with a wedge. Sod coverings of roofs are heavy and recommended only for log roofs. Sod has advantages that it will limit air leaks and provide mass insulation. A better plan for scavenging of roofing is to find sheet metal. Large sheets will cover a roof. Nail holes need to be sealed to keep water out. Also, plastic sheets will work but are temporary.

Flooring: Carpets are hard to make, and they are hard to clean. A throw rug can be cleaned by hanging outside and beating it. Also, leaving it in the sunlight will sanitize it. Hardwood floors are made from leafing trees. Sanding them smooth may be difficult, so rug coverings may be preferred. A mill with grindstones might give you the ability to slowly sand. Lacquer from fir, spruce or sumac trees can seal wood. When distilling the turpentine out of fir sap, the remainders are the lacquer. Spruce and sumac may need thinning with turpentine. For rug making, see cloth.

Windows: An opening can be covered with an animal hide or shutters. Rather than making glass, any thin material might admit light such as a thin layer of an animal horn or a shaving of marble. Pieces are set in place in wood, iron, or lead. Paper can be used to admit light but needs to be protected with shutters during storms. Blown glass can be made into flattened cylinders and then cut pieces used for small panes. Glass takes 2400 degrees to melt. Materials are silica from sand that has been chemically purified. For doors, see woodworking.

Insulation keeps a building warm in winter. The most important factor is sealing air leaks. One hole will let in more cold air than will come through uninsulated walls. Seal walls with plaster. Making a structure with tight quality control will help, but there will still be gaps. Insulation is trapped air pockets. The smaller the air pockets, the better. For example, a hollow wall with no insulation will let in more cold air than an insulated wall because the insulation has many small air pockets. Wood is a good insulator alone, so a log cabin that is well sealed should be easy to heat. Also, straw roofs are insulating if they are thick. If you have a hollow cavity construction, fiber from plants or rags tends to be a very good insulator. Of course, wool is a great insulator, but you may not have enough to spare. If you have sheets of fabric, paper, or plastic, spacing them at one-inch intervals inside the wall will insulate as long as you seal the ends, so the air doesn't sneak around. Alternatives to insulation are cave homes and heavy buildings. Cave homes will stay near the ground temperature which is usually near the average year-round temperature for the area. Heavy buildings are stone and sod homes. These are similar to caves in that the mass surrounding is the structure is so much that it takes a very long time for structure to change temperature. Heavy structures average out the temperature changes over days or weeks but will become very cold in winter.

Plaster can be made from lime, gypsum, or clay. Clay plaster is clay with sand and fibers. Sand is to be sufficient to prevent shrinkage and cracking in drying. Fibers can be straw, grass or extracted from manure of grazing animals. Add lime if you have it.

Carpenter bees are large bees that make holes in old wood. The holes are more than half an inch in diameter. A humane way to get rid of them is to put up wind chimes because they don't like the sound and will leave. Otherwise, plugging the hole would kill any inside and discourage the ones outside.

Carpenter ants are large ants that dwell in wood. They can destroy wood structures like termites. If you see very large ants in and around your wood structures, you may have a problem. Prevent them like for termites. Kill and eat any that you find. They are good source of vitamin C. Remove old stumps near your home. Inspect wood for holes and softness.

Termites: See prevention in the section on construction. Inspect for them by looking for wood dust or for the tunnels they construct along the base of a foundation. Destroy the tunnels and eat the termites. They are high in protein.

Woodworking

Doors, ladders, barrels, furniture, and bed frames can all be made. Pine and alder are examples of soft woods chosen when you want to be able to easily work it. However, when durability is more important, a hardwood like oak is chosen. Cedar is usually soft, but some such as Western Red Cedar are stronger.

Common wood joints should be defined. Most joints can be made with a chisel by repetitively trying to see if it fits. However, saws can help too. Some joints will hold together on their own, but a little glue will help, and some joints will require a connector like a dowel. A dowel is a cylindrical peg that inserts into two slightly smaller holes, one in each piece. The dowel might be a softer wood that is easier to exactly carve and that will precisely fit in holes. A butt joint is just abutting two pieces together, so it requires a connector. An example would be when making a table by butting two boards together side by side. Alternatively, table boards could be grooved so the pieces fit together. A lap joint is like two logs for a log cabin coming together at a corner. In a log cabin, the joint is held together by the weight of the logs. A lap joint could be carved with a dovetail so that the lap expands to keep it from pulling loose. A box joint is for making boxes for furniture. A box joint is made like a dovetail lap so that there are many dovetails along the length of the joint. A mortise and tenon is like a dowel joint, but the tenon is a dowel that is originally a part of one of the pieces and is cut to be exposed. A little glue will help all joints.

Ladders can be made many ways. One ladder is two parallel ropes with either rope or wood steps attached across, but this only works when dropping a ladder. A ladder can be made by tying or jointing shorter branches to be steps along two longer branches. Jointing can be on one face of the ladder, or circular holes can be made for each branch, and they can be doweled into it. A ladder could be made by carving steps out of a log, but then it is heavy to carry. It would be more like a semi-portable staircase.

To get smooth boards, a large saw is necessary. Then wood is typically dressed or sanded down. Splitting wood is the alternative. To split wood, start on one end with a wedge and force it down the length of a log. The split will follow the grain of the wood, but the quality of the split varies by type of wood. This is usually straight enough for clapboards and split rail fences.

A rope bed is a frame of four legs and four beams jointed together. Ropes go between the beams in each direction to support the sleeper. One or two ropes are woven through holes in the frame and loop back and forth across the whole bed. Ropes will slacken with time and are tightened with wedges. In cold climates, because bedding smooths bumps, thicker rope with wider spacing is used. In warm climates, because little bedding is used, thinner strands are woven together to provide even support.

Doors are the most likely location where you will have air leaks. Hinging of doors was first done by having dowels on the top and bottom on one side that stuck into sockets in the door frame. With that sort of hinge, the door would be set in place before the top sill of the frame was added. Without a hinge, the door would have to be lifted out each time the door was opened. A simple door can be made from nailing or tying vertical clap boards to horizontal boards, but it will be very leaky. Door construction was often paneled so thicker stiles around the edges would hold the panels in place. Each piece would have to be jointed to keep the assemblage together. A door could be made like a window, so see options for them. Locking doors from the inside can be just putting a bar across it. Locking from the outside normally isn't a concern in small communities.

Seats: The bench was the most common early piece of furniture to sit on. A single, wide clapboard can have one wide leg at each end jointed into its bottom. To provide sway stability, diagonal pieces could be used as in post and beam construction. A bench with a back to would require vertical boards at the end to be jointed into. A stool was less common because it required more accurate jointing of legs into a base. A stool has sway stability if the three or more legs are at opposite angles and are solidly jointed. A much longer-term way to make a stool with only axes and no saws is to repeatedly chop down a small tree at the desired stool height. It will keep growing back and broadening the stump. Then finally chop out the stool from the ground. With more careful woodworking, other chairs can be made.

Cushioning: Pillows are usually woven and stuffed (see Cloth). However, early pillows were sometimes carved wood. Even pottery has been used as a pillow.

Containers such as buckets can be pottery, sheet metal, or even leather. A wooden bucket is made like a barrel.

Barrels are made of different quality based on what it is to hold. A liquid container needs to be higher quality than a container to temporarily carry harvested foods. Making waterproof barrels requires a high level of skill. Oak is a common material for barrels, but pine and yew are used too. About twenty-four vertical pieces of wood (stiles) need to be made. The stiles are thin enough to bend and are tapered at each end. The flat ends of the barrels are boards that have been jointed together, usually with dowels. Once metal was available, metal bands were used to encircle the barrel and hold the stiles together, but wooden withes (flexible willow branches) were used before. . Only four to six metal bands might be needed, but nearly constant withes would be needed over most of the height of the barrel. Withes were willow branches lapped to make a hoop, and then twine or a smaller willow branch wrapped around was used to hold the lap together. Part of the skill in barrel-making is knowing exactly how much pressure the pieces can take when tapping it all together. Another skill is exactly forming each piece so they fit together with no leaks, but small gaps can be filled. Wax is usually placed along the seams to seal it. A hole is drilled in the middle and closed with a cork.

Metal working

Fuels and temperatures in an industrial oven or furnace: You can tell the temperature of a fire by looking at its color. A match flame is orangish and is 1400 C or 2600 F. Candle flames are normally around 1600 C or 2900 F. A warmish color is 2100 C or 3800 F. Daylight color is 4700 C or 8500 F, but overcast daylight is more bluish. Above 6250 C or 11200 F, the flame starts to look bluish. Iron should melt at 1500 C or 2800 F, copper a little less, and aluminum melts about half that. Comparing temperatures that metal melts at to these flame temperatures, you see that it should be possible to melt a metal pot in a flame, but this doesn't occur because the metal rapidly moves the heat away into other parts of the pot or to the food, so its temperature never rises to its melting point. Therefore, to melt a metal, the whole piece of metal needs to be heated evenly. Fossil fuels are ideal for getting the temperatures. Wood typically can't get hot enough to melt metal but can be made into charcoal. In a forced air furnace, charcoal can burn at 1260 C, or 2300 F. This wouldn't seem enough to melt iron, but iron can be forged at a temperature as low as 900 C. Even down to 750 C, there can be some reshaping of iron. Charcoal is wood that has burned at high temperatures by denying it oxygen. Charcoal can be made in a kiln or buried in a mound under a thin layer of sod or loamy soil. Leaves or straw are often put under the soil. Only small holes at the along the side of the mound are left to provide minimal air and a way to introduce burning leaves to start the fire. Modify holes to regulate burning by moving them down the sides of the mound. Move down when the smoke turns bluish. Large batches for charcoal-making are stacks of wood 20 feet across and several feet high. Tradition is to stack the branches upright, and not use small brush, and to leave an opening or chimney in the middle. There should be very little smoke after it gets going. Expect it to take days to produce charcoal. Plug the small hole when done to extinguish, then spread out charcoal to cool and water any embers. The volume of charcoal will be half or more of the volume of wood consumed. The pile may settle and cracks form in soil, so reseal it. Tar can be produced too if pine is used. See the section on adhesives. Sometimes a clay channel drains the tar out the bottom. Activated carbon is charcoal that has been above 900 C (1700 F) in the presence of steam to cause void formation. Similar to making charcoal from wood, coke is made from coal. Coke is superior to coal for the same reasons charcoal is superior to wood.

Locating ore: Recycling is best is you can find metals. However, ore can be found. Much of the commercially exploitable materials are already used. Yet thin veins still exist. Look in outcroppings. Iron ore is sedimentary, and usually you will see rust-colored bands, but can be dark too. Copper ore can look gold, green, purple or black. Lead ore often looks like silver and contains some silver. Other ores are much rarer.

Smelting: Converting ore to metal requires heating to drive off gases or slag. Coke is often used. The coke is burned producing carbon monoxide which reacts with ore to remove oxygen and produce carbon monoxide. Iron ore will convert to iron at 1250 C which is below its melting point. Recycling of metals doesn't require removal of oxygen unless it is significantly rusted. Slag is lighter or heavier than iron so can be drained off in layers. After the ore is converted to iron, it will typically have too much carbon, and that will make it brittle. Therefore, to make steel, carbon is removed by adding oxygen. To get the right carbon content, a blacksmith can adjust the working of the iron, so it absorbs carbon again from the heat sources. Very small amounts of other metals can be added to steel to improve it such as copper. Copper may be smelted in pottery kilns. Copper is mostly available as sulfite minerals which are smelted to make copper. Bronze is copper with one-eighth added tin. Tin is rare but can be gotten by smelting Cassiterite.

Forging/blacksmithing: Shaping of iron can be done by putting the iron into a pile of burning charcoal that is driven by a fan to force air through it. Once the desired temperature is reached, the metal is pulled out and quickly hit with hammer or anvil to shape it. Reheat it to make it hot again. A yellow-orange color of the iron is considered the ideal temperature for forging. Iron or steel is often heat- treated after it is near its final shape. One type of heat working is quenching and tempering. Hot metal is quenched in a bucket of water, so it suddenly cools. This will make it harder. Tempering is reheating, but not as much, so that some of the harsh effects of the quenching is released. Tempering is more important for tools. Generally, fine points and edges are desired to be hardened so they are strong, but interior portions of metal parts are desired to be tough which is more flexible and the opposite of hard. Copper and bronze don't respond to heat treatment but will harden with cold working which is bending or tapping on it after it is cold. Since these metals may have been worked before, recycling them by reheating them may lose beneficial properties. The recycled metal may have to be reworked.

Saws: For stone saws, see stone hand axes. Make the cutting edge serrated. For metal saws, see forging/blacksmithing. Saws have been made from copper, bronze, and then iron. The blade is made into a sheet by pounding, sometimes more than worker simultaneously. Then teeth are punched out. Thin saws can be held straight by a wood frame or with a folded backing strip of steel. Hardening is important for saw life.

Fasteners. Nails are made one at a time by pounding iron into a wedge shape. Blacksmith nails will be thicker than common modern nails.

Water

The body can adjust to some organisms in the water, and they might actually be healthy for you. However, some organisms are really

bad. Minor organisms in well water are usually the okay ones after
you adjust to them, but river water has the bad ones. Keep soil out
of wells because it has bad microorganisms. See water treatment in
Mid-term survival.

Security

See Hunting for weapons.

Some dog breeds are better at being guard dogs. Some of the best
are pinchers, terriers, and German shepherds because they bark
loudly. See also home security in mid-term survival section.

Food and Hunting

Hunting

Hunt from downwind. Animals will smell you and run away unless they have been acclimated to the smell from living nearby. For example, squirrels growing up in the wild will be more cautious that the ones in your front yard. If hunting by walking, go upwind from your starting point so you will always be downwind.

Throwing sticks can be used to hunt small game. A boomerang is a type. Boomerangs for play return, but those for hunting fly straight. Typically, it is just a stick with a heavier end. They are easy to find or make and so may be the first tool to be made in a hurry. It may have a sharpened end to maximize penetration if it flies straight, or a sharpened edge for slicing if it spins. A throwing knife is an advancement but requires metal.

Bola means balls in Spanish. It is a cord five or six feet long with weights tied on the ends that are a few inches in diameter. Sometimes one end of the cord is split with two balls. It is used by swinging around by holding one end and then releasing at the neck of large birds, to entangle legs of large mammals, or to cause injury from direct impact to bones. Used in combat, there are many variations of swinging, whipping, throwing and slamming down. A lasso is also a snaring weapon. It can be used to rope the neck of animals.

A sling is a hunting tool or weapon. It is a cord with a pouch or split in the middle to hold a projectile. It is swung overhead, and one end of the cord or handle is released to send the projectile to the target. The cord can be a total length of four to seven feet depending on desired range. The handle ends may be different for easy release of one end. The size of projectile varies by purpose. Small bullets have been made with holes for poison to use in combat. To increase range and power, one side of the cord can be replaced with a long wooden staff instead.

Spears are long pointed poles that can be jabbed or thrown at large prey. Spears vary in length depending on the purpose. Smaller, closer game require shorter spears. For safety, spears should be at least your height up to two feet longer, otherwise carry in a hard case. Choose a straight sapling to make the spear. When thrown, a tail is necessary to keep the spear straight on target. Using a spear-thrower increases the power of the throw. A spear-thrower is short shaft with a cup. The back of the spear rests in the cup. The thrower is about the length of a forearm regardless of spear length. Finger loops may help to retain it in-hand. A spear with a cord attached to it is an amentum. It functions as a tail and can be used to increase throwing power like a spear thrower, but the thrower stays attached. When spearfishing, barbed tridents increase the success of catching and keeping a fish. To catch fish, aim below the target due to refraction in water.

The tip of the spear is fire-hardened wood, bone, rock such as flint, or metal in a triangular shape. To tie points onto the spear, split the spear or arrow cutting across the grain, leave notches in the point to tie it on, and add glue if you have it. Bone points will break if you miss and hit something hard. You could smash rib bones of mammals until you find a suitable piece to grind down. Flint is a sedimentary rock. It often has a darker color inside if you break it. With experimentation flecking (flaking) along the edges, you should be able to make a point. Start by smashing up the rock and finding small pieces. You can test any sort of arrow tip to see if tempering helps. A can lid can be folded over a few times and smashed flat with a rock each time to make a tip. Break off excess at end. A fire-hardened point only needs to dry, not to singe. Pre-treating it with an oil might help protect it. While hot, burnish by pushing down hard with a rock by scraping motions.

A bow and arrow set is difficult to make but has better range than a blow dart gun. However, if you want power at long range, a spear with thrower might be better. A bow requires a high-quality string which is hard to make. See thread making in a separate section. To make arrows, see spear making. Reeds or thin saplings are good if straight, a quarter inch wide and at least two-foot long. Bending under heat can make the arrow perfectly straight. To make a bow, select a sapling that is straight hardwood, has five or six feet without branches and is an inch or two thick. Choose the best side to be towards the target and leave that side alone if possible. Trim off the side towards you until the bow starts to be bendable. Use finer detail to smooth it and then make the tips. Both tips should feel equally flexible. Make notches for the bowstring on the side of the tips. Slant the notches down. String the bow and check the symmetry. When under proper tension, the bow should be bent about six inches. Arrow fletching or feathering is very difficult. Duct tape is a temporary last resort. See glue instructions separately if using feathers. Feathers should be split down the quill. Make the quill wet before tying the ends to the arrow with sinew. Then apply glue to the length of the quill. Additionally, wrap the quills to hold them tight while glue is setting. Wrap with a thin thread by splitting the feather to insert the wrap. Then remove wrap and preen feathers.

Using working dogs is an alternative way to hunt. Dog breeds such as hounds are bred to chase down prey the size of racoons. Larger game could be cornered by these dogs then shot. Smaller dog breeds are suitable for squirrels. A dachshund is useful with all burrowing animals. Setters, spaniels and pointers will point to birds, but you would need a way to shoot them when flushed. Dogs are sometimes persistence hunters. They take turns chasing a prey for hours until it is worn out.

Wild animals are more likely to have anthrax. See notes in health and livestock sections. Check the killed animals for signs so you know the risk level in your area.

Fishing and seafood:

Limit consumption of river fish because of mercury. Mercury is everywhere because of smoke from coal plants. Fish that are big or live a long time accumulate more mercury because they eat more. Smaller fish are safer. Shrimp, salmon, tilapia, pollock and catfish have low mercury levels. Most shellfish are relatively low. Children and child-bearing women should have no more than one serving a week, but others can have two. Temporarily eating more, and then less later should be fine except for child-bearing women.

See spearfishing above. Net fishing may make sense in some areas if fish school or migrate. Fishing with line requires a string, hook and bait. Hooks can be carved from bone. Put barbs in your hook so the fish won't come loose. Fishing line can be any cordage. Bait depends on the fish, but worms can be dug, and other bugs found under logs and stones. A simple rod from a tree branch gives you leverage.

Fish like resting in still waters. If you put a cage, in still waters, fish may go into it. Then you just pull the cage from the water.

To prepare a fish: Scale by scraping against the grain of the scale if you eat the skin. Otherwise, you may peel the skin instead before or after cooking. When filleting, a glove helps. The basic filleting method is to cut behind the front fin towards the head on a diagonal until reaching the spine. Make a shallow cut on that side of the spine until past the top dorsal fin, then cut fully through and scrape as you go. Repeat on other side. Fold back and use gentle sweeping cuts to work around the ribs. Repeat. Check the head for meat before discarding. You can skin the fillets now by putting the fish skin-side down and using a scraping cut. For each type of fish, you can adjust your method.

Other seafood: Clams, oyster, mussels, and scallops look similar. Some are buried in mud, but others attach to a substrate. A pitchfork is usually used to dig in mud or sand in flats. Swimming may be necessary for attached types if it is high tide. Crawfish like water with stones because they need them to hide under, and the water has to be clear so they can hunt. To catch by hand, carefully sneak up behind and grab the tail. Move some rocks around if you don't see them.

There are too many other types of seafood, and each has a special way to be caught. It is too much to list them all in a guide focusing on the northern US.

Sealed and stabilized modern gunpowder, such as in a bullet may last 50 years. Also, it can be manufactured. As long as you have metal tubes and projectiles than you can have functioning guns. Gunpowder requires saltpeter, charcoal and sulfur in the proportions of 15, 3 and 2. If the gunpowder is for blasting or other uses, it can have lower amounts of saltpeter in proportion. See the section on minerals for sulfur. Charcoal is discussed related to metal working. Charcoal from softwood is preferred for gunpowder. Modern black powder also includes other ingredients such as a graphite coating to reduce the chance of static electricity causing misfire. Saltpeter is potassium nitrate. From bat guano, soak the guano in water a day, then evaporate the water to get saltpeter crystals. From urine, run livestock or human urine through a sand pit. Later leach out nitrates with water. The nitrates need to be converted to potassium nitrate, and can be done by filtering through potash. For potash, you can use wood ash. Crystals on cave walls may contain nitrates. However, you may need to process it in different ways. If it is

calcium nitrate or contains much magnesium, you need to process it
with potash.

Farming (including grains)

Plowing: Plowing breaks up native vegetation. It can also mix in
compost. Without a plow and team, you need to turn over soil by
hand with shovels, hoes, pickaxe or a simple digging stick.
Alternatively, pigs will turn over soil. Plows can be pulled by
horses or oxen, alone or in teams. Water buffalo, donkeys and
camels have also been used. A simple plow from wood is a yoke to
tie to animal, a beam from the yoke to the handle, the stilt (handle),
and the share (blade). The share can be made of metal, stone, or
even a stick. Simple plows can't handle any obstacles such as tree
roots or rocks. A digging stick is a sharpened, hardened stick that
may have a broad handle. A simple plow made with a stick for a
blade might be enough to cut a furrow for planting but not enough
to turn soil. It is custom not to plow or plant in soil that is too wet
because conventional wisdom is that working the soil then will
compact it.

Seed preparation: Some seeds need to be prepared. Others can be
started in greenhouses. Higher value plants are sometimes started in
greenhouses, but usually not grains. Starting in greenhouses can
make plants productive earlier in season, or it can lengthen a
growing season in a colder area. Some seeds need to be soaked.
Fruit seeds benefit from soaking in warm water for one or two days.
Alternatively, seeds with thick cases may need to be scratched to
break the case. This mimics the effect of passing through an
animal's digestive system. If disease is transferred with the seed,
then seeds can be washed in water that is very warm but not hot
such as 50 Celsius or 120 Fahrenheit. If potting soil holds disease,
it can be pasteurized at the same temperature for 15 minutes. Some
seeds need to experience freezing temperatures in order to
germinate.

Timing: Seeds germinate at different soil temperatures. Greens
typically germinate at very low temperatures but vegetables at very
high temperatures. Frost can stunt plants that are not suited to the
cold. Seeds that haven't come above ground yet are protected by
the soil. If starting vegetables inside greenhouses, you should
harden the plants as you bring them out. Seedlings will be
accustomed to indoor temperatures and sun levels. Bring them out

by exposing them more each day to sun and cold until they are ready.

Planting: Seeds are normally planted at a depth of two to three times the seed size. A sharpened pole can be used to make the hole. Small seeds could be broadcast across the ground and then left as is or worked into the ground by gentle raking or harrowing. Forest seeds often need to be on the surface and to see direct sunlight to germinate. Grains are often planted at a rate of 100 kg or 220 pounds per acre which is 209 feet in each direction. This is because smaller, lighter seeds produce smaller plants so can be closer together. Seeds prefer various conditions such as types of soil and water.

Fertilizing: The world is covered in barren land that was once farmed. Farmers have removed all of the nutrients from the soil and not replenished it. To restore barren land, compost waste to have perfect balance with nature. Use urine immediately and feces after treatment. All materials such as minerals and nitrogen will flow back to the ground. However, you need to sanitize the waste. Either waste can put in a compost pile or methane digester. Both need to get to between 130 to 160 degrees F. After two months, it is safe. Waste put in the ground is considered safe after two years, but that is not true for all infectious diseases. For example, anthrax is known to stay in the soil for ten years. The most common nutrient that soils lack is nitrogen. Beans and clover fix nitrogen which means they take it from air and put it in the ground, so planting beans and clover cover crops is an alternative to urine/feces fertilizer. However, land could be lacking any mineral. Other common minerals lacking in ground are phosphate, potassium, and zinc. Ash, especially from maples, is a good source of potassium. Each could be added, but using waste provides the perfect material balance.

Harvesting: A sickle had a medium handle with a hook at the end to cut grain by pulling. Sickles can be made from metal or long pieces of flint. Also, individual pieces of flint were attached to a wood or bone handle. The flint teeth are held sin place by resin. A scythe is another way to cut. A scythe has a long handle to make it easier to stand while cutting. A scythe has a curved blade and is swung along the ground as the body rotates. The handles are often wood and that blade metal. Sometimes additional grips extend off the handle for each hand at the end and about a third to half of the way down. The blade could be made from other materials if necessary.

Threshing and winnowing: thresh seeds or grain or bean loose from chaff by beating them on the ground with a flail which is like long nun chucks. It is probably faster than shelling by hand. You can drive animals in a circle around and over some grains to thresh. Some seeds thresh easily by walking on them. If you can make a threshing machine, you can power it with a crank, pedals, a water wheel, or horses on a circle. You want a rotary system of beaters. Scavenging an antique thresher might be easier than making one. Putting through a roller might be enough to thresh rice. After loosening seed from the chaff, next is winnowing. Wind will blow loose chaff away if you shake the mixture. Dropping from higher will give more distance in lower wind. Winnowing may also remove some pests.

Storage: Grain can be stored in dry pits. An above ground silo can be made from a domed or conical brick structure. To keep pests out, you want to seal the silo. Silos have possible hazards of collapsing grains, lack of oxygen and toxic dust. Grains, especially ones high in oil content, may spontaneously combust if improperly stored. If grains are stored in humid conditions, they are more likely to ferment and build up heat. This also occurs with hay and compost.

Milling to flour: You can grind grain with a mortar and pestle. Animals walking over grain will crack it, but not grind it very well. Grinding stones can be rubbed over a base stone. Mills can be powered by hand, animals, wind and water. A large circular mill stone rotates on top of a base stone. The millstone usually had a fan pattern of indentions to grip grain. Non-traditional ways to grind are with two rotating stones that come together to push grain between them, and having a rotating drum filled with hard balls such as metal.

Livestock

Chickens for eggs or meat: You need a rooster to have fertilized eggs so you can grow more chickens. Laying chickens live about three years. They will always lay three eggs, and when you take one, the hen will replace it in a day. Pull one out each day and you might get five a week. Chickens eat bugs, but when that isn't enough, feed them sweet corn, sunflower seeds, pumpkin seeds,

mint, cucumbers, sweet potatoes, kale and chickweed. Incubator
temperatures need to be 99 to 100 degrees which is hard to do, so let
the hens raise the chicks.

Goats for milk or meat: Goats live twelve years and eat clover and
grass. They often need a mineral lick for salts. In winter, you can
feed them hay from grasses. Keep goats away from plants toxic to
humans.

Pigs: Pigs will eat fallen apples and reeds. In the wild, they eat
leaves, roots, fruit and insects, but farmed pigs are usually fed grain.
Pigs are easy to raise if you can fence them in an area large enough
for natural food, protect them, can feed and shelter through winter
and give a lot of water. Each drinks gallons a day. Also they can
help till ground for farming.

Livestock eat about 3% of their weight per day. To calculate the
food required for storage, large animals weigh about 500 pounds for
a cow to 1000 pounds for a large horse. Goat weights vary by breed
from 100 to 300 pounds. Mature sheep weigh about 300 pounds. A
cow could be kept with the grass of an acre or two depending on the
productivity of the forage. Animals could require much more area
in dry western grasslands. Proportion up or down based on the
animal size. One acre is 43560 square feet. Livestock need about
one gallon of water per day per hundred pounds weight. If they are
working animals, they eat and drink more.

Bees: When bees swarm, they are sending out half the colony to
start a new one. Have a box ready for them to move into, and now
you have your hive. Catching wild bees is much harder than
splitting an existing hive because you don't know if you are getting
honeybees. Many other stinging insects may find your hive before
the honeybees. Out of 20,000 species of bees, only six are
honeybees. If you are getting your bees from splitting, then you can
probably get the knowledge, too, of how to raise them from the hive
owner. However, if the owner has moved away you need to know
more. You can trace bees back to their hive by first feeding them,
so they are full. Try to feed several bees at once so you have more
to follow and time their return. When they leave, record the time
and direction. A twenty-minute return is one mile. Hives will be
horizontal or vertical. If you find an abandoned hive, get the
previous owner's protective clothing, too. The face and neck are
most important to protect, but you may go without gloves if
confident. If you get stung on the hand, you can remove the stinger

quickly to limit the venom transfer. Scraping off the stinger is better than pinching it which may force in more venom. Washing the stung spot with soap is also helpful. Fresh onion or leek juice helps. Wash clothing frequently because bees will mark their scent on it as an enemy. Smoke calms the bees. Smoke is produced from incomplete combustion. Green pine needles are a good source of smoke. Sumac (staghorn not poison) is another option. The body can build up tolerance to poisons, such as bee venom, that produce immune response. Being stung regularly can reduce the reaction to it. Immunity does not develop to non-immune poisons. Beehives are generally put in the shade near sources of water. Honeycomb is often spun to extract honey, but you can eat the wax comb too. Crushing and straining is an alternative to spinning. When harvesting honey be extremely careful not to disrupt the queen. Some hives have screens that keep the queen in one segment of the hive. Smaller worker bees will fill the whole box with honey. Some cells of the comb are honey, and some are bee larva. It is okay to eat larva if you must, but it damages the hive. Don't extract too much honey because it is the hive's winter storage food supply. Harvest in June and September, and more if the colony is doing very well. Wait until the hive looks about 80% full. From a healthy hive you can get 25 pounds per harvest. Leave two-thirds of it for the bees, or more in colder regions. Capped honeycomb cells are healthier for you. In cold regions, you may want to insulate the beehive in winter to keep it warmer.

When caring for livestock, be careful of anthrax. See health for diagnosis and treatment in people. The bacteria are in some wild animals. When those animals die, the bacteria can stay dormant in the soil for decades until livestock eat grass where the animal died, then they become infected. Then handling of the livestock can infect the caretaker. To limit the infection of livestock, don't release animals to the open-range; free-range in large pens is better. Keep wild animals away from livestock feed. When culling animals of any type, follow safe handling methods. Never eat an animal that looks sick. Instead dispose of it in a place that won't be used by animals in the future, or burn it. Check the skin for black lesions. Modern grazing animals were vaccinated against anthrax. Pets aren't likely to get anthrax because they don't eat grass but could eat infected meat. Pasteur vaccinated livestock by variolation. See human infections for the general process. The problem with the Pasteur method was how to weaken the bacteria enough so that it didn't kill the animals that were vaccinated. He exposed the bacteria to oxygen to weaken it. Under a microscope with purple gram staining, the anthrax bacteria, which is 1 to 9 micrometers long, looks like rods.

Fencing can be done with a split rail design. See woodworking for splitting timbers. A split rail fence could be a zigzag of piles of wood stacked alternatingly on top of each other. Improvements are to support it at the joints, make a straight fence by piling between two posts, and jointing the pieces into the single post.

Shepherd dogs protect your livestock from predators. There are many breeds that are suitable to be sheep dogs. Generally, large, loud dogs are good. Start training when only a few weeks old so they imprint on their herd. It takes until the dog is two years old for it to be reliable. If you are in an area with large aggressive predators, you may need to protect your dogs with wide, thick leather or even spiked collars around their neck where predators attack. Smaller dogs like corgis and collies or any heeler might not be as good at protecting the herd but are better at keeping them together. For animal care, see rabies under infections. Brushing your dog's teeth will prevent excessive saliva production which might falsely make you concerned that they have rabies. Train a dog to be social with people. Expose it to people and situations. Train your dog so it is easier to control. Treat with positive rewards. Be sensitive to your dog. Spaying male pups may keep them from being aggressive, but then most working dogs use aggression to hunt, guard, or protect livestock.

Foods

Vermin-scaping is farming worms, crickets, meal worms, grasshoppers, beetles, or moths. Use a container that they won't escape from. Put the bugs inside the container along with a food source. Keep the temperature above 50 degrees to keep the vermin active. Ideal soil or biomass temperature is 70 degrees. Crickets eat food scraps or spoiled foods. Earth worms eat mulch or compost such as a mixture of grass and leaves. Be sure to water your bugs.

Weeds can be eaten. See a list of weeds and so forth at the end. These foods might not be providing much more than variety.

Trees:

Trimming trees is best done when the tree is dormant if it is one you want to keep such as a food tree. That minimizes trauma. Try not to cut away more than one-third of a tree in a year. The best time to cut an invasive or unwanted tree or vine is yesterday.

Propagating fruit trees and vines: Nearly all foods that people eat are hybrids. This means that generations of wild plants are bred together to produce seeds for a bountiful crop. For example, in corn, a wild variety with sweet kernels might be bred with a variety with large kernels to produce large, sweet kernels. Therefore, using seeds from one generation to the next won't produce the parent crop, but random pairings of desired and undesired traits. Fruit trees such as apples, and vines such as grapes, likewise may not produce as bountiful of progeny. However, grafting can be a way to reproduce the same tree or vine. Grafting is taking a part of a tree or vine and connecting it to a new stump of a compatible species. For example, by taking vine branches or buds from a good grape vine and placing it on a wild vine, the new vine will grow. Many new trees and vines can be produced that way. To produce the most progeny, bud grafting is recommended. A single bud is removed from the source and put into the recipient. With any grafting, the cambium from the new and old have to be in contact so the old can feed the new. Once the bud has become successful, begin pruning back the rest of the plant to encourage the bud to grow. Grafting helps to get fruit trees to bear fruit more quickly. Trees often take 5 to 9 years to bear fruit, but grafting a fruiting branch onto a young tree can make it start to bear in 2 years. See trimming above.

Baking

See ovens elsewhere. Breads made with phragmite starch are more like biscuits or cookies.

Baking soda is a chemical leaven. It is sodium bicarbonate. It is produced from mined carbonate deposits like soda ash. Soda ash is found in desert regions in dry lake beds. It can also be made from limestone and concentrated salt water in a complicated process.

Baking powder is another chemical leaven. It is usually an acid and base mixed that won't react until in water. It is commonly sodium bicarbonate with and acid such as cream of tartar, and corn starch mixed in to keep them from reacting.

Yeast is a biological leaven. You can capture wild yeast and make a sourdough starter.

Wacky cake is an easy recipe that doesn't require butter or eggs, although it does need a leavening agent. Mix 4 cups flour, 2 cups water, 3 cups sugar, 2 tsp baking soda, 1 cup oil, 2.5 tsp baking soda, 2 Tbs vinegar, 2 tsp salt, and flavoring such as 1 tsp vanilla and 6 Tbs cocoa. Without industrial baking soda, you may have to use yeast. Bake in a 9x13 pan for 30 minutes at 350°F.

Preservation

Storing food in a basement is good for the cool temperatures. However, basements sometimes flood. Build storage to take boxes off the ground, or make sure every container will float.

Apple preservation: Apples can be made into cider as discussed above (see fall fruits). Also, they can be dried, made into sauce, or buried whole.

Dried apples: Dry by cutting thin. Thinner takes less drying time. Optional is putting in vinegar water to keep color. String on a wire or string and hang sideways. Keep a small space between each slice. Readjust spacings over two days to keep each piece drying well. May need to take in at night or to cover to keep bees away, but you can try it without. Should be dried to leather feel but to preserve well you might want to make it into a chip. Alternatives to aid drying are solar ovens. An alternative to stringing is to lay flat. Apple leather is the same, but you can add spices to the ground apples.

Burial preservation: It is possible to use the ground as a refrigerator. The ground usually never gets very warm if you are away from the equator. You could experiment with burying foods deeply to preserve them. You should bury below the frost line if you are going to keep the food well into winter. Most years the frost line is not as deep as the maximum of roughly four feet in northern US states. The frost line is the depth of foundations for buildings without basements. Be careful the area is well drained since you don't want the food to go under water. To handle sporadic water, a drainage layer under may help. A concern with this method that one bad apple spoils the whole lot. If gases build up from one decomposing apple, it will affect the others. In addition to apples, roots, cabbage and salted meat bury well. Sometimes food was covered with straw or leaves. Don't mix different foods in the same hole. Check regularly. Map or mark the food location.

You can indirectly dehydrate. If you put food in the sun, some vitamins won't be preserved. A thin cover of clear polycarbonate can filter UV. Also, closing it like a solar oven will make it go faster. You need air flow to get out the moisture. Herbs just need to hang upside down to dry.

Dehydrated vegetables: Most vegetables will dry. Blanching briefly in boiling water will kill enzymes that could shorten life. Some, like tomatoes, are best stored in oil.

Fermentation is a preservation process. It converts sugars, which easily would spoil, into other foods such as alcohol or lactic acid, in the case of milk. Fermentation occurs as the result of the growth of beneficial bacteria cultures. Varieties of cheese and yogurt are produced from milk by the actions of different bacteria and methods. Pasteurization is sometimes done which is to briefly boil the milk to kill bacteria. Inoculating with a starter culture ensures that the fermentation will be with the beneficial bacteria. This gives the good bacteria have a head start on any other natural bacterial. Identifying a good starter can be a matter of chance if you have none available.   Fortunately, in some foods, the natural bacteria are the beneficial ones. In the case of apple cider, the beneficial bacteria are normally much more present than any other bacteria, so no starter is necessary. See the fall fruit section about apple cider. Leavening for bread is yeast. Yeast for bread may be easy to find, and then kept going with starter. Milk is fermented into cheese or yogurt. Fruits and grains are converted into alcohol or vinegar. Vegetables are picked into relish. Beans are fermented. Cottage cheese is made from milk that is put in an animal's stomach or salted. Grazing animals have rennet. The rennet enzymes in the stomach curdle the cheese. Some people waited for the milk to sour first before making this. Cheese is first made by curding cheese with rennet or an acid like vinegar. Then curds are drained and pressed to dry them. Alternatively, before coagulation, milk may be warmed so that lactic acid naturally forms, and then less other acid is needed to be added to curdle it. The initial step is when a starter is added if you are going to add one. The starter will give it a specific characteristic of cheese. Next, curds are sometimes warmed to promote whey to run off and they are drained overnight. Finally, many cheeses are ripened or aged in many different conditions of temperature and so on to give it distinctness. Aging can last weeks or years. Salt stops aging because it halts microorganisms. Beans are often fermented with filament fungi from decaying vegetation such as rice straw or hay. Also used is old bread that may have small mold. Beans are boiled, and then kept warm for a few days after inoculation. Then beans are quickly dried or eaten.

Beer is fermented grain. When malt is desired, the first step is malting which is steeping grain water to wet it, germinating for a few days, and then drying to stop germination unless it will be used immediately. Keep the germ from getting too hot. All grain is milled/ground and then mixed with plenty of water to make mash. Mash should get warm or hot from enzyme action and may need heat to get started. After a couple hours, the liquid is drained. The remaining solids are sometimes used as livestock feed, but it is edible for humans too. Next, the liquid should be boiled for an hour with any flavorings like hops. Boiling does many things such as kill undesired bacteria. To brew, it is cooled to room temperature and then inoculated. Brewer's yeast is thought to originally come from grape skins. Starter from good batches can be kept. Beer should be filtered now with remnants kept as starter. The beer is then aged in bottles or barrels for weeks to years in a cool place. Often a little unfermented liquid is added so that bubbles will be produced in sealed bottles.

Wine: Remove the grape stems which taste bad. Wash away spider webs. Gently crush the grapes. Yeast is already present and visible on the grape skins, but sometimes yeast is added to make the result more predictable. Wine should stay at a cool room temperature while fermenting. To judge if it has fermented, taste it. After fermentation drain the liquid wine from the solids. Optionally, press grapes but this is lower quality wine. If you have precipitation on the sides looking like sand, it is cream of tartar which is an acid. Next, chill the wine in a wine cellar for a week or two. An optional step is fermentation in sealed containers with lactic acid to reduce bitterness. This can take months. Wine will become clear, and the lees can be filtered. Put in sealed bottles or oak barrels so that the air doesn't oxidize it. Normally, it is aged for a couple months or more. Spoilage is unpredictable and hard to prevent without preservative. Sanitary practices and storing wine as cold as possible deter spoilage.

Salted meat is sometimes referred to as a fermented product, but it is not fermentation. Salt or brine is added to meat to kill all microorganisms. Additionally, you often should press meat, such as seafood, to extract as much water as possible. The salt concentration should be 20% or higher in brine. Ocean seawater exceeds 3%, so would need a 7 to 1 reduction. Fresh surface water in rivers and lakes would have to be reduced to less than a percent of its original volume. As an alternative, you can measure the weight of salt to add to freshwater, so it is 20% by weight. Meat is usually soaked before eating to remove the salt. Save the extracted salt for reuse. Botulism is possible if not properly salted. The common symptom of mild botulism is drooping eyes. Inability to breathe is the second symptom and requires a mechanical ventilator. Recovery from botulism is in 2 to 8 weeks.

Distilled alcohol is pure alcohol. Alcohol will boil at a lower temperature than other liquids, therefore the steam is pure alcohol. Capture that steam in a condenser. Steam rises, so at the top, route a side tube through a bath of cold water. Angle the side tube down so that it drips into a collection container. Some other compounds that easily evaporate may be collected too and will provide flavor. Food alcohol may have to be used for medical purposes since wood alcohol is much more technically difficult to produce.

Vitamins and minerals

Eating a varied diet usually provides sufficient vitamins and minerals. However, if you are planning to preserve foods for winter, pay attention to each of these so that you keep a balance during that time. These are traditional foods below, but some vitamins and minerals have been discussed throughout this book. Salt, iodine, fluoride and chloride are examples discussed above. Below, each list is usually ranked from highest to lowest vitamin/mineral strength. Unlisted vitamins and minerals are normally not a problem.

Vitamin A: Dehydrated carrots or sweet red peppers, or liver.

Thiamine/B1: Whole grains, legumes, pork, yeast and fruit.

Riboflavin/B2: Milk, eggs, leafy vegetables, meat, beans, mushrooms, and almonds.

Niacin/B3: Yeast, peanuts, bacon, sunflower seeds, mushrooms, and almonds.

Pantothenic acid/B5: Dairy, eggs, potatoes, tomatoes, oats and sunflower seeds.

B6: Whey, liver, meats, peanuts, spinach, mushrooms and various potatoes.

Biotin/B7: Organ meats, eggs, fish, meats, seeds and nuts.

Folate/B9: Yeast, poultry liver, peanuts, sunflower seeds, lentils, chick peas, spinach, soybeans, broccoli and other nuts.

Cobalamin/B12: Shellfish, liver, bacteria, fermented foods, eggs, milk, and seaweed.

Vitamin C: Dried sweet peppers, dried chives, and the fruit of the rose plant.

Vitamin D: Sunlight on bare skin causes this to be made. However, in winter, supplement with fish bones, or mushrooms grown in direct sunlight.

Vitamin E: Vegetable oils, nuts and seeds.

Vitamin K: Fresh parsley, kale, leaf vegetables, carrots, grapes, tomatoes and potatoes.

Choline: Egg yolks, organ meats, soybean oil, bacon, chicken, shell fish, cauliflower, broccoli, oats and beans.

Calcium: Dairy, fish bones, soy beans, and kale.

Chromium: Broccoli, grapes, and cured turkey meat.

Copper: Sunflower seeds, liver, seaweed, dried mushrooms, and oysters.

Iron: Any meat including eggs, raw yellow beans, soybeans, spinach, ginger and lentils. Try for a mix of both meat and plant sources.

Magnesium: Pigweed grains, rice grown in peat or clay and especially including the bran, hemp or cannabis seeds, barley, yogurt, pumpkin seeds, beans and spinach.

Manganese: Cloves, chickpeas, whole grains, leafy vegetables and nuts. Seafood has it, but that may be only because it is a pollutant.

Molybdenum: Legumes, grains, nuts and seeds.

Phosphorus: Most protein sources have it.

Potassium: Dried parsley, tomatoes and sweet peppers, milk, nuts, soybeans, potatoes and greens.

Selenium: Nuts, eggs, oysters, meats and grains.

Zinc: Meat, fish, shellfish, eggs, and dairy. Vegetables can be high in zinc if not grown in sand. Those include: rice, beans, nuts and seeds.

Wild foods

Some of these have been discussed earlier. More detail is given here. Often there are sub-species that have similar descriptions and appearances. For example, wild strawberries come in many varieties.

Reed: Remove starch from rhizomes and use as a sugary flower. Sprouts are best before the leaves form. Eat raw or cooked. Sprouts taste like cucumbers and licorice. Tap cattail pollen over a bucket for a protein. Cattail flower spikes are like corn on the cob. Phragmite and cattail roots can be cooked like potatoes but have high fiber. Roots are best when plant is dormant. Too much phragmite root and cattail pollen may have a sedative effect.

Bulrush is a type of sedge that grows on edges of water. Roots are edible. Bake or make into flour. Identification: It is like tall grasses. Nut grass is a shorter version of sedges. Flowers vary significantly between species.

Greens: Fresh greens are fine raw or cooked. If there is a chance that a wild animal carcass decomposed there in the last several years, you would have to cook greens. When choosing garden areas, be cautious if you see evidence of dead animals.

Chicory roots can be roasted. They have blue flowers with square fringed tips. Best in autumn. Roots can be fresh or dried. Too much can be a laxative or increase urine flow.

Figure 18. Chicory

Locust: Black locust pods are dark brown. The seeds are brown beans that are flattened. Seeds are edible after cooking. Since I am uncertain if boiling destroys toxins or simply leaches them, throw away boiling water. Honey locust pods are reddish. The pulp is edible too and should taste sweet. If the seeds are undercooked, it might have a narcotic effect.

Queen Anne's Lace: Bouquet of white flowers looks like lace. Its root is an edible carrot. Some people may be allergic to the root. Also, touching the leaves could be irritating. Root increases urine flow.

Clover: Dutch white clover has three leaves and a white head. Cook or put leaves on salad, heads go on salad raw. Can be dried for humans and animals but be very careful never to eat moldy leaves. Roots may be eaten but are small. Other clovers likely taste bad if poisonous.

Food Oil: Rape seed, part of the mustard family, is used to produce canola oil. It grows wild in fields. Canola is specifically bred to reduce the erucic acid which is not easy to measure without lab equipment. (It is the lighter weight fraction oil.) The acid appears not to be much of a health risk to heart unless consumed exclusively. The plant is a few feet tall, has yellow flowers with four small petals in each flower. The pods are shaped like a shriveled string bean. Seeds inside are dark purple and round.

Seeds can be used as a source of protein in fodder. Mustard seeds
are yellow and can be used the same way for oil or to eat seeds fried
or ground but are spicy. Flowers are likely to be bell shaped. Black
mustard has flowers that are half an inch wide, leaves a couple
inches long, and a small pod that is four-sided. Garlic mustard has
leaves that are triangular or heart-shaped, toothed, makes a garlic
smell and slender pods. Some species of mustard allergens are
poisonous to livestock, so do a poison/allergen test before using any
wild plant. Sap often tastes spicy. Oil can also be made from okra
seeds, dogwood seeds, winter squash, and beech and other nuts.
Also, see nut grass under antibiotics because its oil is preferred.
The first-year nut-grass plants might have very small root nodules.
If you are farming them, let it grow a few years. This is a plant that
is worth farming. Grape seeds can be made into oil, but they are
very high in tannins, so the oil has to be refined using alcohol or
acetone. Ginkgo biloba seeds are edible if cooked otherwise they
are mildly toxic, and it is a source of oil.

Figure 19. Nut grass.

Juneberries or Serviceberries: If you can identify them, they grow
easily and produce edible fruit. There are many sub-types. It is a
bush or tree with a rounded crown and white flowers. Bark is gray
or black and furrowed. Mature fruits are in clusters and can be red

or dark purple. Fruits are round and smooth with a small number of seeds. Tastes like apple.

Groundnut: Tubers are one to two inches. Eat raw or cooked. Taste like sweet potatoes. Plant in the sun or light shade in loose soil and protect against slugs by crop rotation by dividing a tuber or sprouting seeds by soaking in water for a couple hours, then putting in soil for a couple months. Tubers increase in size for three years, so let it grow if you can and harvest in fall. Easy to store through winter. Seed/bean and seedpod is also edible. Identify: find on edges of woodlands, especially in wet areas with sandy soil. It is a vine. Flowers are warm colors and unusually shaped (Bell or hood-shaped. Looks like hearts with tongues coming out.). Look for tubers near the surface by pulling on a root. Tubers look more like widening of root than other tubers like potatoes.

Hawthorn is in the same family as plums. The fruits are the size of a cherry or larger and come in many of the same colors as plums, but red is the most common color. Identification: Often a small, flowering tree. Bark is smooth and gray. Most have thorns on the branches. Has five stones stuck together in a clump in the fruit. It lowers blood pressure, so don't eat exclusively.

Try the leaves and seeds of mallow plants. Don't use modern fertilizer on mallow.

Hog peanut is more common in on sandy or chalky soil, and in moderate shade of a thicket. It produces two types of seeds. The buried legumes are larger. Tastes like peanuts. Buried beans are one per round pod. Flowers are pinkish.

Milkweed can be made edible. Since it is widespread and easy to identify, you might explore this. Use only the newest growth of shoots, leaves, buds and flowers. Must be boiled a few times and discard water to remove toxic bitterness. Avoid dogbane, which has stems, because it is more poisonous.

Figure 20. Milkweed

Stinging nettle leaves can be eaten. Use only the youngest leaves.
Harvest with gloves. Cook to eat, or dry preserve, and that takes the
sting. Laxative if too much is eaten.

Duck potatoes can be preserved through drying. Find in wet areas
and in water. Leaves are large arrowhead-shaped. White flowers.
Roots are white, but tubers are purple. Tubers may be a couple feet
from base of the plant, but not too deep in the soil. Tubers are best
harvested in fall. Cook like potatoes. Peel after cooking. It tastes
like chestnuts.

Russian Olives are invasive but are widespread. They are short
trees and have narrow, silver leaves. Fruits look like rough-skinned
green or tan olives. Wash the fruit, and then chew and suck out the
fatty cream. Spit out the pit and hard skin. If it tastes bad, don't eat
it because it is likely too early in the season, or maybe too late.

Pigweed is the source of amaranth and quinoa which is a popular
grain. Harvest seeds before they drop. Will need to thresh and
winnow tiny seeds but threshes easily. Young greens are also edible
boiled. Don't fertilize pigweed with modern fertilizers and eat in
moderation. Identification: Up to six feet tall. One main upright
stem but can branch. Flowers are on long narrow spike at top.

Leaves alternate and are 2 or 3 inches long and wide on relatively long stems/stalks. Seeds are tiny and black. Tumbleweed is a type of pigweed.

Figure 21. Pigweed.

Lamb's Quarters: Preferred for pleasant taste. Boil leaves or dry for later. Best leaves are young ones from an old plant. Seeds should be easy to collect. Identification: Two feet tall. Leaves and stems pale or whitish, and leaves are large and roughly triangular.

Purslane is also called hogweed, but the nickname confuses it with pigweed. The most common type in the northeast is a common weed. Eat the leaves, stems and seeds either raw on salads or cooked. It is a good source of oil. If collecting seeds, let them dry over a tarp, then shake loose, and funnel into a jar. Identification: Purslane grows across the ground with pink stems. Leaves can vary significantly between species, but the one grows as a common weed in northeast has leaves that are light green paddles. See the figure. Some purslane leaves are fleshy and succulent. I am unaware of any poisonous plants with succulent leaves, so try succulents.

Figure 22. Purslane

Ramps are wild leeks. Looks like an onion on the bottom, but the tops are long leaves. Find in spring on streamside. The color from bottom to top is white, purple, and green. Eat the whole plant. Spicy.

Many or possibly all cress have edible leaves. There are too many distinct species to identify here. If you want a bitter green for variety and recognize cress, try it.

Thistles are any flowering plants with prickly leaves. Most leaves can be eaten if spines are removed. Roots and stems are edible if you boil and remove spines.

Raw velvet leaf green seed pods can provide a source of protein and oil. Alternatively, collect ripe seeds, wash if too bitter, grind and cook.

Figure 23. Velvet Leaf

Spice berry: Mostly for flavoring. Dry red berries and use like all spice. Alternatively, make leaves and twigs into tea.

Figure 24. Spice Berry

Linden berries: Linden trees are bushes with very large round leaves. Berries are usually red. Fruits should taste sweet and have a single large seed.

Figure 25. Linden berry

Figure 26. Burdock

Figure 27. Blackberries

Hazelnuts are round nuts that are two-toned. Eat when they are green or ripe. They will store for a year. Can be made into oil.

Lotus is an aquatic plant. Leaves are nearly round. Soak roots in warm water if they are bitter, and then cook them. Roots are best in autumn. Seeds are tasty. Young stems and leaves can be boiled.

The American persimmon grows in the eastern US and has a small orange fruit.

Autumn olive is a bush with small red fruits. It is invasive and spreading. Identify by silver scales under leaves and small silver spots on fruits. Harvest after berry is fully ripe in late autumn for best flavor.

Stickwilly or cleavers is a low weed that sticks to clothes. Pick early in the year and boil it. Can be slightly irritating.

Daisy roots can be eaten raw. Young leaves can be boiled.

Foods particular to the southern US:

The Jerusalem artichoke is a wild sunflower more common in the south. Boil the roots or eat raw.

Maypops or purple passion flowers are more common in the south. The vine produces a seedy fruit with a little edible pulp.

Kudzu is an invasive vine that is common in the southern US. The root of the kudzu plant is a potato. The flowers, and young leaves and stems can be boiled.

Garden snails are edible if they are well-cooked.

The black persimmon is found in southern Texas.

Marsh marigold roots must be very well cooked to remove natural poisons.

Sassafras trees may be more common in the south. Leaves have three different shapes from oval, mitten and three-pronged. Small amounts of leaves can be boiled or eaten raw. The toxins aren't usually harmful except in large amounts over a long-term.

Foods particular to the northeastern US:

Basswood or Linden tree: Young leaves can be cooked or put in salads. Eat sparingly since excess amounts because of tannins and other compounds.

Food in coastal areas:

It is best to forage at low tide which is when the moon is at or just below either horizon. When the tide is out, start looking for fish, shrimp and crabs in puddles. If you plan in advance, you can leave a heavy container to make an artificial puddle. Birds are attracted to the shores too at this time, so you can hunt them.

In muddy shores such as river estuaries, look for worms, clams, crabs and burrowing snails. Crabs may be walking around or they may be in a hole. The holes may look like tiny puddles, so poke them to see if they are deep. For big crabs, a long hook may help get them out of the hole. A net can help you get crabs that are walking. A bow and arrow may work on large, fast crabs.

Finding beach worms takes practice. In the shallowest water, as a wave is receding, put some rotten bait in a bag and whip it along the water on a string to get the scent out, look for a tiny head coming out of the sand, let it grab the bait, grab the head softy with pliers or firmly with thumb and finger, dig around it in the sand or mud until you can get a firm grip, then gently pull it out.

In sandy shores, some of the same foods are below the sand. Clams and scallops: Dig clams at low tide. Look for the squirting of water out of the sand to locate them. A tube may be a fast way to extract a column of sand. Spread the sand to find the clam. Separate from shell with a knife. Remove inedible parts. Scallops are on the surface of the ground underwater. Using a snorkel and mask is the easiest way to find them.

Burrowing snails can be found by running fingers through the sand or mud.

In rocky shores, looks for sea snails, crabs, sea cucumbers, mussels, oysters, sea lettuce, gutweed, sea squirts, shrimps and prawns, and dog whelks.

Sea lettuce, seaweed, gutweed and kelp are edible green algae growing in the water. It that looks like red or green leaves or grass. It is eaten raw or cooked. It is a source of protein and vitamins. Not included is sea grass. Sea grass is distinguished from lettuce in that it has roots that look like those from any land plant.

Mussels are in groups on rocks. Use gloves and wiggle loose. Purge mussels of sand by washing. Clean them by rubbing them together. Steam until then open. Oysters are harder to spot. Pry them off and open with butter knives or screw driver and hammer. Some eat raw, but fry them.

Sea cucumbers can be found in shallow tide pools. They look like tubers, but can be any color. Split open and remove guts. Roast over a flame until well-done.

Sea squirts are tubular and fixed to the bottom like sea cucumbers, but live in colonies.

Hermit crabs are small crabs that live in shells. Just pick up the shell to catch it. Put them into boiling water. When cooked, they will be easy to pull out of the shells. You can eat them whole.

Sea snails: Periwinkles, welks and Limpets. Scrape them from rocks with a rock or knife. Wash and soak the snails. Winkles are shaped like land snails. Limpets are conical. Cook limpets on coals until they are loose in their shells. Boil winkles for 10 minutes. Dog welks have similar appearance. Welks produce red and purple dyes. Cook like winkles.

Shrimp or prawns: You may see them swimming along the rocks on in shallow pools. You can use tongs to grab them by the tail. Throwing a weighted net into the water is another way to catch some.

The beach plum is common in sand dunes along the US northeast.

Greenbriar or Smilax grows in tropical areas. Is a climbing plant commonly found in dunes. Fruits in late summer.

Young leaves or shoots from beachside succulents are good raw or cooked.

Foods in arid western US:

It is best to migrate out of arid areas. However, some food will be available to sustain you on your journey. Valleys and creek or wash beds may have more life in them. In arid areas, plants are likely to have stronger flavors to discourage animals to eat them. Some foods like stinging nettle would never be on the top of the menu in other areas, but may be one of the necessary choices here. Stinging nettle should be steamed or fried.

See previous mentions of lamb's quarters, dandelions and wildflowers.

Check for seeds, nuts and fruits if the season is right for them. Fruits from some cacti such as saguaro and cholla are edible. The stem or pad of cholla is edible raw or cooked. Singe the hairs off cacti. See notes above about prickly pears. Most fruit seeds have cyanide.

Young leaves of Miner's lettuce are edible raw or cooked. The plant is short. Each stem ends with a leaf. Leaf's change shape with age. On older leaves, the stem goes through the middle of a leaf which is actually two leaves.

The piñon is the type of pine found in arid areas. Look for seeds.

Juniper trees might be found in arid areas. Fruit is harvested in the fall. Since they are mildly poisonous, you should only eat a couple per meal. Eating too many will cause digestive symptoms.

Tepary beans are orange, brown or black.

Mesquite bushes or trees have bean pods. The pulp is edible.

Ironwood trees are often the tallest in the desert. They have small green leaves, purple flowers and light gray bark. Eat the green peas or cook the dried ones.

Palo Verde trees have green bark and yellow flowers. The flowers are edible. Cook the beans. If you have a bitter plant, soak the beans and discard the water before cooking.

Chia seeds grow in the chia plant. The dry flowers can be harvested to remove seeds. It will be difficult to hold the sharp dried flower without gloves. The flowers are clusters at the tip of the stem or along it.

Devil's claw has green triangular leaves with five lobes. Stems are sticky, curved and have white hairs. The bitter fruit is edible.

Wolfberry is a type of goji berry. Different varieties of the plant exist. Most commonly they have purple flowers. Fruits are bright warm colors.

In arid areas look for mushrooms, amaranth, oak trees, squash and sumac. See previous instructions for these foods.

Burrowing animals can be caught by putting snares over their holes. See the squirrel pole concept.

Foods particular to western mountains:

See the section on food in arid regions. Many foods in mountains are the same as elsewhere. For example, see harvesting of sap from Aspen trees. A variety of berries can be found in mountains.

Fireweed is common in many mountain areas. It has purple flowers, red stems and leaves that alternate. Flowers are edible. Young shoots and leaves are edible raw or cooked. The root can be roasted. Older stems can be peeled. Some say large servings cause stupor.

Deer are common in mountain areas.

End Notes

The stories also by this author may contain additional details about these methods and materials.

Disclaimer: The author assumes no liability for any instructions in this book.

About the Author:

Nick Eager is a pseudonym for the author. Nick lives and works in Michigan. He has professional experience with planning for various disasters.

Contact him at: https://www.facebook.com/nick.eager.395

If you enjoyed this book please loan it to a friend, or write a positive review of it.

Summary:

This is a guide for surviving many types of disasters. The information is provided in a calm manner. It has no scary hype, but clear facts. Written by the author of exciting but realistic stories of a possible apocalyptic scenario.

The guide covers the extensive information to help you solve your problems related to food, water, shelter, security, health, and long-term quality of life after those things are no longer available. The three sections cover short-term, mid-range, and long-term survival. Those sections correspond to what you will need to know for the first month, the first year, and for many years afterwards.

The shelter information focus on colder locations. The food collection information emphasizes urban, suburban and rural areas in northeastern North America.

"I am a murderer." That thought had kept running through my head for the last couple days. I had tried to focus on work, but the word "murderer" kept taunting me.

Looking back, that first month after the solar flare had knocked out the power was rough. We'd lost everything of the old world, and we had no water or food supply. Few people were left in town because most people had fled south. The few that were left were really desperate, but it was too late to leave now with there being no way to get anywhere. I had survived by making tough choices. It had been so hard for me that I feared how it had affected me. Several people had died, and I was responsible for at least one of the deaths. At times, all I did was sit and think about each person who had died and how I'd killed them or contributed to their death in some way.

I was troubled by the death of my friend, Jason. He had been caught in circumstances beyond his control. I told myself that he didn't know that the others had been planning to burn down his church. I should have been able to come up with a way to get him out safely, but I'd barely escaped myself. Since then, I'd come up with an alternative theory. I'd been so concerned with getting out that I hadn't thought of the others. Instead, when I saw the arsonists, if I'd turned back and yelled "fire," then a large crowd might have rushed the men with me. We could have overpowered them. It was so simple, so why hadn't I thought of it?

"No," I told myself. I must stop the blaming myself and refocus on the positives.

My family was all doing fine. Ann and Frank were helping to harvest the food we needed, and Lily was helping in her own way. Ann's elderly father Ron was still with us and did some physical labor even though he had a bad shoulder. Yet, he was needing less pain medicine for it each day. Frank seemed to be adjusting to the new life the easiest, so I was least worried about him. He'd had a few issues early, but he reminded me of when I was young. As a child, I hadn't gone through a major trauma like we all had recently, but just like him, I pushed through whatever life gave me.